NAMES OF ANGELS

NAMES OF ANGELS

C. FRED DICKASON

MOODY PRESS
CHICAGO

© 1997 by
C. FRED DICKASON

All Scripture quotations, unless indicated, are taken from the *New American Standard Bible,* © 1960, 1962, 1963, 1968, 1971, 1972, 1973, 1975, 1977, and 1994 by The Lockman Foundation, La Habra, Calif. Used by permission.

Scripture quotations marked (ASV) are taken from the *American Standard Bible,* © 1901 by Thomas Nelson & Sons, © 1929 International Council of Religious Education.

Scripture quotations marked (NKJV) are taken from the New King James Version. Copyright © 1979, 1980, 1982 by Thomas Nelson, Inc. Used by permission. All rights reserved.

Scripture quotations marked (KJV) are taken from the King James Version.

ISBN: 0-8024-6181-6

3 5 7 9 10 8 6 4

Printed in the United States of America

CONTENTS

INTRODUCTION

They are all around us, involved in our personal lives, popular culture, and even the world scene. And yet they are unseen. They are the object of fascination for ages and yet recently broken upon us in faddish delight. They are angels.

Angels are mysterious beings, not limited to our atmosphere, not governed by our physical laws, not totally understood by human minds. Most important, they do exist, and they have an impact on our lives.

As a new millennium approaches, bookstores carry many shelves or whole sections devoted to angels. Magazines have published feature articles devoted to angel themes and even to purported sightings. Though long an interest in the world at large, the subject of angels is approaching epidemic proportions in America.

This curiosity about things angelic reflects a greater interest in things spiritual. The July 8, 1996, cover story of *Newsweek,* for example, says America is hooked on the paranormal. UFOlogy, out-of-the-body experiences, shamanic soul-travel, channeling, psychics, meditation, crystals, telepathy, ESP, pycho-kinesis, witchcraft, and vampires are conjuring up curiosity and infecting our society. Tired of what the material world offers, people are attracted to supernatural and paranormal concepts and practices. And, as usual, there are those who are cashing in on it; movie producers, authors, counselors, and even business consultants reflect our interest in the spirit world. The Internet has already attracted a crowd of dabblers. Even the White House has had leaders who consult psychics and occult counselors.

Most of the public are unaware of the dangers of demonic deception. As we consider the names of angels, it's important to realize there are angels, good and evil. One-third of the angels fell with Satan (Revelation 12:3–9), which means humans are open to deception with regard to angels. The Bible indicates that these fallen angels are demons, evil in nature and practice.

Instead, many advocates of the power of angels claim all angels are good and are on earth only to help people. Some occult practitioners claim to be channelers for messages from angels who would offer secret power to enrich our lives. Elizabeth Clare Prophet, leader of the Church Universal and Triumphant, has advertised direct dictation from various high ranking angels. Some years ago Prophet conducted her angels seminar at the North Shore Hilton in Chicago. She claimed she spoke the words of Archangel Gabriel ("a dictation"), in a special revelation, after she had lectured on "How Angels Help You to Recapture the Spirit of Joy." "How Angels Help You to Create Miracles in Your Life" was her precursor to another dictation, allegedly from Archangel Zadkiel. Archangel Raphael and the Blessed Mother followed her lecture on "How Angels Help You to Heal Yourself, Your Family and Friends." Holy Justinus and Seraphim with Angels of Victory supported her lecture on "How to Work with the Angels for Success." During the seminar she also promised "The Sealing of the Servants of God in Their Foreheads: Third-Eye Blessing with the Emerald Matrix."

What is the truth about angels? The Bible, the revealed Word of God (2 Timothy 3:16; 2 Peter 1:21) actually speaks of only one archangel, Michael (Jude 9), though he is called "one of the chief princes" (Daniel 10:13). And only three angels are specifically named: Michael, Gabriel, and Lucifer. The Bible clearly describes fallen angels as those who chose to rebel with Lucifer (now called Satan) against the only true and living God (Ezekiel 28:12-19; Matthew 25:41).

As the great deceiver (Revelation 20:2–3), Satan now leads other fallen angels. They blind the minds of those who do not believe the gospel of the Lord Jesus, the Son of God. Evil angels, or demons, hinder the service of God's true servants. They pose as messengers of light, but they are counterfeiters with wicked intent. They design to lure the unsuspecting to indulge in false religions and to seek to gain secret knowledge and tap secret power.

Such evil angels would love to turn our interest from the Creator God to angels. They would be glad to imitate God, to pawn themselves off as messengers from God, to capture our attention with their activity, and to divert our worship and trust to creatures with destructive powers. Of course they use good bait, promising success, health, and happiness with the wisdom and power they would share.

But the price is too high! Promising life, they deliver death. Promising riches, they deliver spiritual rags. Promising health and wisdom, they deliver spiritual (and often physical) sickness and deception. The crucified and risen Lord Jesus labeled Satan a murderer and liar from the beginning (John 8:44). The apostle Paul warns against their blinding and deception (2 Corinthians 4:3–4; 10:3, 13–15).

We must know the truth about angels. *Names of Angels* will encourage you with the truth about God's good angels, His messengers and servants who help us in the privilege of serving Him. It also will warn you about the evil intent and goals of Satan and his demons. We will learn their limits and our resources in God's Son, Christ Jesus, and rejoice in prayers of thanksgiving and supplication for the help of God's holy angels.

We need to guard ourselves and to be ready to help those who are seeking truth but following the lie. Where are you in this current interest in angels? Have you given it a thought? Does your concept of reality include the realm of personal spirit beings that affect your daily life and the course of world events? Do you have a criterion to evaluate the truth about angels, good and evil?

Names of Angels will acquaint you with the names of angels, good and evil, so that you might appreciate their creaturely marvels, their activities, and the genius and power of the God who created all of them through our Lord Jesus Christ. (The larger picture of what the Bible says about angels is the subject of my book *Angels, Elect and Evil* [Moody Press].)

It is my hope that you will enjoy and profit from this study and gain insight into practical applications of the truth involved. May we become better prepared to worship the Lord of Hosts, who created us and an innumerable army of angels.

Chapter 1

WHO ARE
THE ANGELS?

We all look at the world through colored glasses that affect how we view reality. Those glasses are called our worldview. The Bible—the divine revelation of God—informs us about the truths of our earth and the God who created it.

A complete biblical worldview recognizes the reality of God, the Creator; and of angels, good and evil, who are created and finite spirits.

Angels are among us. As we will see, they are personal beings with intellect, emotions, and will, and they have a distinct nature.

Angels: Their Reality

Praise the Lord! Praise the Lord from the heavens;
Praise Him in the heights! Praise Him, all His angels;
Praise Him, all His hosts! (Psalm 148:1–2)

We all view the world through colored glasses that affect everything we see. Those glasses determine how we perceive reality and the structure of the world; they affect how we see people and events. The colored glasses are called our worldview. Not only does our worldview determine how we interpret our world, but also what we think is valuable. It determines our choices and direction in life.

A complete biblical worldview recognizes the reality of God, the Creator, an eternal and infinite personal spirit being. It also holds that there are angels, good and evil, who are created and finite beings. The whole spirit world—God, good angels and evil angels (Satan and his demons)—interact among themselves and with human and natural life. Those who deny or minimize these realities have an incomplete worldview and are open to misinterpreting facts, events, and experience.

But God is real, angels are real, and demons are real. They all affect our lives and the world in which we live. There is much biblical evidence for that. Human experience has also borne this out.

The word for *angels* occurs 108 times in the Old Testament and 165 times in the New Testament. The Bible narrative does not present a continuous scenario of angelic activity, but angels do have significant interventions and interactions with one another and with humans.

In thirty-four of its sixty-six books, the Bible writers mention angels: seventeen in the Old Testament and seventeen in the New. The Bible classifies angels as either good or evil. The good are "chosen" (1 Timothy 5:21) and "holy" (Matthew 25:31). They worship and serve God faithfully and energetically (Hebrews 1:7).

Evil angels include Satan, their chief (Matthew 12:24–26), and demons (Matthew 25:41). They oppose God and His servants, human and angelic. These two armies carry on a great battle that surpasses human thought and affects the life of individuals and nations.

This reality should not be confused with animism or dualism. Dualism holds that there are two equal and opposite forces that constitute reality and sometimes clash. (Zoroastrianism and the oriental Yin-Yang are representative of this view of the world.) Instead the Bible pictures God, the Creator of all, the unrivaled sovereign of the whole universe, as allowing and supporting all life. No creature can survive without Him. He uses good angels as His servants to aid His people (Hebrews 1:14). They administer some events in nature and in human affairs.

We can take heart that no individual, human or angelic, can succeed in opposing God. After God has allowed and limited the willful expression of evil, He will end the careers of sinners and judge them.

Father God, Creator of heaven and earth, let me understand the reality of Your world. I want to view properly the spirit world and its wonder and activity. Let me see how all Your creation reflects Your wisdom and power, instruct me in truth, and keep me from error. Amen.

Angels: Their Personhood

*And when He again brings the first-born into the
world, He says, "And let all the angels of God worship
Him."* (Hebrews 1:6)

All angels, or spirit beings, the Bible says, were created
by God through His Son, the Lord Jesus Christ
(Colossians 1:16). He created them for His purposes and granted them all sorts of privileges and characteristics.

They are *personal beings.* They were created to
have fellowship with God and each other. To enjoy
this privilege, they must be persons as God is a personal God.

As created spirit beings, they have no material
bodies. But these unique beings have *personal intellect.* They can think in the moral realm, as seen by
their understanding of God's holiness and worthiness (Hebrews 1:7; Revelation 4:8–11). They also
desire to investigate the marvels of Christ's redemption of humans through His sacrifice on the cross
(1 Peter 1:11–12).

They have *personal emotions,* seen both in awe
and reverence of God and in their rejoicing when a
sinner repents and trusts the Son of God to save
from sin and guilt (Luke 15:10).

Their *personal wills* allow them to choose to
obey and serve God (Hebrews 1:14) or rebel
against Him. Angels who remained true to God re-
spond positively to the command to their wills to
worship Christ (Hebrews 1:6). Satan and one-third
of the angels chose to disobey their Creator (Isaiah
14:12–15; Revelation 12:3–4, 7–9). Satan and his
demons willfully seek to deceive humans regarding

the truth in Christ to prevent their salvation (2 Corinthians 4:3–4; 11:3, 13–15).

If we understand that personhood is the essence of the image of God, we may infer from biblical evidence that angels, as humans, (Genesis 1:26) were created in God's image.

Thank You, Father God, for creating me in Your image. It causes me to marvel to think that You have created many spirit beings also in Your image—persons who can relate to You. I want to relate to You properly with the intellect, emotions, and will You have given me. Draw me to Yourself. Let me appreciate more Your holiness and worthiness, and let me enjoy all that for which You created me. In Jesus' name, amen.

Angels: Their Nature

Are they not all ministering spirits, sent out to render service for the sake of those who will inherit salvation? (Hebrews 1:14)

How may we further describe angels? How are they constituted by the Creator? The Bible states that they are spirit beings with certain powers and that they are directly created by God.

They are *spirit beings.* They have no material bodies, though they may appear to us as humans or in other forms as allowed by God. They have no weight or physical dimensions (Hebrews 1:7, 14). But they do have limitations in space, time, and strength. They can be in only one location at once, even though they may move swiftly (pictured by wings). One angel, sent by God to Daniel to reveal His program for Israel, was delayed for three weeks in transit by the opposition and strength of an evil angel called "the Prince of Persia." Michael, one of the chief princes of God, was sent to wrestle with the evil prince to relieve the messenger (Daniel 10).

They have *certain powers.* God gave angels power in the material world. They sometimes affect human life, helping the righteous in acts of ministry (Acts 5:17–20) and opposing the wicked (Acts 12:23). They may at times, under God, control earth's elements, such as the wind and the sun's heat (Revelation 7:1; 16:8–9). They also carry on warfare with one another (Daniel 10:13; Revelation 12:7–8). One day, at Christ's return to earth to reign, one angel will bind Satan to cast him into the abyss (Revelation 20:1–3). Good angels may also be involved in the final defeat of Satan and his armies of demons, casting them into the Lake of Fire (Revelation 20:10; Matthew 25:41).

We need not fear the power of God's angels. Their powers are granted by God and governed by God. Furthermore, the good angels are devoted to our welfare.

They are *special direct creations of God.* Since angels don't procreate nor die (Matthew 22:30; Luke 20:36), and since Christ created them all before the foundation of the world (Colossians 1:16; Job 38:7), they come directly from the hand of God. How wonderful is God's creative genius! Each angel is different, just as snowflakes. There are millions of angels, perhaps trillions (Revelation 5:11). These beings endowed with great intelligence and powers, constantly worship God as Creator (Revelation 4:8–11). We can take their example to heart. We also owe all that we are and have to God. We exist and enjoy life and breath by His sovereign creation and gracious will.

Lord Jesus, I know You have created all things, visible and invisible—all angels. I seem to have a hard time thinking about persons without bodies. I'm so limited in my human way of thinking. Expand my concepts so I may see more of the reality that You have created and that exists right around me. Thank You that even though I don't comprehend all this, You know all, control all, and care for all, including me. Amen.

Angels: Unredeemable

For assuredly He does not give help to angels, but He gives help to the descendant of Abraham. Therefore, He had to be made like His brethren in all things that He might become a merciful and faithful high priest in things pertaining to God, to make propitiation for the sins of the people. (Hebrews 2:16–17)

Good angels need no redemption, for they never rebelled and are not guilty and lost. They were given grace to withstand the temptation to rebel with Satan. They are called "elect" (1 Timothy 5:11). Fallen, evil angels cannot be redeemed. The angels are not a race; each angel is a direct creation from God, and each has no relations and no equals. The angels have no one, such as our Kinsman-Redeemer Jesus, to pay an equivalent penalty in their place. Thus Satan and his angels are lost forever and headed for the Lake of Fire.

Good angels worship God for His unfathomable grace in redeeming lost sinners of the human race. They can't understand why God would go to such unreasonable length to save guilty, rebellious men and women. They stand amazed that God actually sent His Son, His equal, His best, to purchase us through His all sufficient sacrifice to become His children and reign with Him upon the earth (Revelation 5:9–10). Angels continually magnify God's grace in sending the Lord Jesus to become the Lamb of God who takes away the sin of the world

How much more should we, who have trusted Christ and experienced the saving grace of God in Christ, worship and praise His amazing, outrageous grace. May we give ourselves to constant, repeated praise and thanks to Our Great God and Savior.

God knows each one of us by name, as He does the angels. All His personal creatures are very valuable to Him. But we have a privilege that angels do not have. We who have received the Lord Jesus as our personal Savior can enjoy God's personal relationship and fellowship. He has loved and rescued us from an eternal punishment, renewed our spirits in holiness, and restored us to Himself. Fallen angels know no relief from estrangement and the ruination that will come to them in God's righteous judgment.

Have you made sure that you, as a special and valuable person, have asked the Lord Jesus to become your personal Savior? When you do, you can know your personal creator God as your Redeemer, Your Friend, your Father. That is a relationship that fallen angels cannot enjoy and something holy angels cannot thoroughly understand.

Dear Father of our Lord Jesus, I am astounded at the grace You offer to fallen humans like me. You sent your Son to be born a genuine human while remaining fully God. Thank You, Lord Jesus, that You humbled Yourself, bypassing angels, to become one of us. You became our Kinsman-Redeemer so that You could pay for human sin. I affirm that I am trusting You and You alone for my personal deliverance from judgment, for my forgiveness, and for eternal life right now and forever. Amen.

Chapter 2

NAMES OF
GOOD ANGELS

Names in the Bible are meaningful. The names of God, of Christ, and of the Holy Spirit are a gold mine for understanding their personhoods and relationships. Their names also help us to understand their actions. The same is true for the names of angels. There are many names for good and evil angels. We shall consider the names of the good first. As we do, we shall learn of the structured hierarchy (ranks) of angels. And we shall find instruction and occasion to praise God.

We begin with five of the more familiar names:

- Angels
- Ministers
- Hosts
- Chariots
- Watchers

Angels

And of the angels He says, "Who makes His angels winds, and His ministers a flame of fire." (Hebrews 1:7)

The name *angel* reflects the Greek word *angelos* (plural *angeloi*). It is also the translation of the Hebrew word *malak*. In each language, the basic meaning is "messenger." Though the word may be used of human messengers, such as those sent by John the Baptist (Matthew 11:10), it more frequently is used of spirit beings, who attend upon God and are employed as His messengers to humans (Luke 1:11; Psalm 104:4). Hebrews 1:7 describes them: "Who [God] makes His angels winds, and His ministers a flame of fire."

The Greek word for winds is *pneumata*. It can refer to breath, wind, or spirit. It seems that the Holy Spirit, who governed the choice of words in Scripture, was playing on the double meaning of the word. Angels, who are spirits, are swift as winds to do the will of God, and winds often fan "a flame of fire," the second description from nature. The fire imagery describes their burning desire to serve God with fervency.

How challenging these God-given characterizations of angels! These spirits, endowed with great wisdom and power, are fully dedicated to serving the true and living God. They know of other so-called gods (described in 1 Corinthians 8:5), who are really fallen angels or demons (1 Corinthians 10:19–20; Psalm 106:35–38). But they choose of their own will to worship and faithfully carry out His orders (Psalm 103:19–21).

Ought not we, who have been redeemed by the blood of the Son of God, to love and trust the One whom angels revere and trust? Let us be swift to serve Him with the fire of devotion according to His Word.

Lord Jesus, You made all angels and humans like me. I owe You all that I am and have, my very existence. Let me, like Your angels, serve You as Your messenger with fervency and faithfulness. Amen.

Ministers

*Who makes His angels spirits, His ministers a
flame of fire.* (Psalm 104:4 NKJV)

The psalmist declares that angels are ministers. The
Hebrew word is *mishrathim*. Like the Greek word
leitourgous (pl.), it conveys the idea of those who
minister as attendants to God. *Leitourgos,* used in
the New Testament, refers to a servant or minister in
religious duties. We get the English word "liturgy,"
referring to an order of service, from this. This
word refers to priestly duties, such as the apostle
Paul considered his appointment by God "to be a
minister of Christ Jesus to the Gentiles, ministering
as a priest the gospel of God, that my offering of the
Gentiles might become acceptable, sanctified by
the Holy Spirit" (Romans 15:16). The risen Christ
now is a high priest in heaven, a minister in the
presence of God for us (Hebrews 8:2).

Though angels do not represent anyone to
God, they do minister as attendants in His presence.
They bring the sacrifice of praise and thanksgiving
to God. They proclaim His worth, holiness, and
power. They may even present some prayers from
believers to God as a kind of incense (Revelation
8:3), though they do not pray for us as Christ does.

We are appointed believer priests to offer to
God spiritual sacrifices in praise and thanksgiving
to Him and in practical service to others (Hebrews
13:15–16). We may have ministries similar to the
good angels, but ours is in a different realm with a
much greater relationship. We are born-again children of God, and we may serve Him out of grati-
tude for our great salvation.

Lord Jesus, You have saved me and called me with a holy calling—to be Your minister. I have a relationship to You and a position that no angel can have. I am Your servant bought with blood. I cherish that relationship and calling. As a believer priest, I offer to You first myself and then my powers and possessions. Let me serve others out of love for You. Amen.

Hosts

Who is this King of glory? The Lord of hosts, He is
the King of glory. (Psalm 24:10)

Angels constitute an army of followers and warriors
in spiritual warfare. This is the emphasis in the
Hebrew term *sava*. God is called the Lord God Sab-
baoth, or Jehovah of Hosts, the leader of a vast army
of angels that goes to battle for truth and righteousness. There are no defectors in God's army of elect
angels. They steadfastly carry out His battle plans
and receive His support in the fray. In accomplish-
ing God's will, they are seen as a means of extending
His power and providence in the governing of the
universe.

Our sovereign God works all His will and de-
feats all His enemies in heaven and earth (Psalm
89:5–10). Assisting Him are the angelic hosts. The
warrior David challenged and defeated Goliath in
the name of the Lord of Hosts. He knew the battle
was the Lord's (1 Samuel 17:45, 47). A "multitude
of the heavenly host" appeared at the birth of the
Lord Jesus (Luke 2:13).

How reassuring to know that angels surround
us at God's command and carry on battles unseen
to protect us! They serve God and His own in a
hostile environment. These well-disciplined and
ordered armies serve Him and us when we sleep as
well, and at other times when we are unaware of
their presence.

Sovereign Lord, I know that there is no god to be
compared with You. Though many invent gods, they are
no gods at all; and I do not fear them. Thank You for the
vast army of angels that serve You and guard me, even

when I don't recognize them or sense the need of Your protection. I would join Your army to stand for truth and righteousness. In Jesus' name, amen.

Chariots

The chariots of God are myriads, thousands upon thousands; The Lord is among them as at Sinai, in holiness. (Psalm 68:17)

Elisha and his servant were "holed up" in Dothan for some time. He had been frustrating the King of Syria. Every time the king would make a military move against the King of Israel and his army, Elisha would warn Israel of the danger. When Syria's king learned of Elisha's counteraction, he sought to capture him. He sent horses and chariots to surround the city.

One morning Elisha's servant woke to find the army circling the city. He fearfully informed his master, "Alas, my master! What shall we do?"

"Do not fear," Elisha answered, "for those who are with us are more than those who are with them." As recorded in 2 Kings 6:17: "Then Elisha prayed and said, 'O Lord, I pray, open his eyes that he may see.' And the Lord opened the servant's eyes, and he saw; and behold, the mountain was full of horses and chariots of fire all around Elisha."

King David declared, "The chariots of God are myriads, thousands upon thousands; The Lord is among them as at Sinai, in holiness" (Psalm 68:17). The *chariots* are angelic armies that accomplish God's purposes. Their intervention brought victory over kings and armies (verses 12, 14).

In a vision from God, Zechariah saw four chariots that carried out God's military judgments on the nations opposing Israel. They were "four spirits of heaven, going forth after standing before the Lord of all the earth" (Zechariah 6:5). Fast moving chariots were feared and effective in battle. And so are angels.

How encouraging to know that God is our protector and that He sometimes uses the swift intervention of angels to protect us. They are present and active even when we are unaware of them. God uses them, in part, to do what the Lord Jesus taught us to pray: "Deliver us from the evil one" (Matthew 6:13 NKJV).

Thank You, my heavenly Father, that Your angels are ready, powerful, and swift to do Your will. I'm glad for their protection, not only in the past but right now. I may not see them as chariots surrounding me and my family and friends, but I know You send them when we need them. I call upon You to send them to keep me safe and to deliver me from pitfalls and harm that the Evil One would bring upon me. In Jesus' name, amen.

Watchers

For His dominion is an everlasting dominion, and
His kingdom endures from generation to generation.
All the inhabitants of the earth are accounted as noth-
ing, but He does according to His will in the host of
heaven and among the inhabitants of earth. (Daniel
4:34b–35a)

Kingdoms come and go. Rulers rise and fall. Who
really rules the kingdoms of this world? Yes, Satan
is called "the prince of this world," but God is the
sovereign. The hymn writer put it well: "And though
the wrong seems oft so strong, God is the ruler yet."
Several ancient kings found this out the hard way.

One king learned this from the mouth of a
watcher, an angel sent to observe, declare, and en-
force God's plans. Nebuchadnezzar, King of Babylon, had a dream that only Daniel could interpret.
It involved a sentence of deposing the king from his
throne and causing him to live and eat like an ani-
mal for seven years.

The king later explained: "I was looking in the
visions in my mind as I lay on my bed, and behold,
an angelic watcher, a holy one, descended from
heaven" (Daniel 4:13). Nebuchadnezzar understood this deposing as involving angelic pronouncement from the Most High God (4:2).

The angel declared, "This sentence is by the de-
cree of the angelic watchers, and the decision is a
command of the holy ones, in order that the living
may know that the Most High is ruler over the
realm of mankind, and bestows it on whom He
wishes, and sets over it the lowliest of men" (4:17).

God has entrusted to certain angels the super-
vision of world affairs. They carry out His decrees

in certain realms. Governments do not exist without God's permission. They may be overthrown at His will. God is the Most High God, the sovereign. It may seem strange to those of us so tied to the material and human world; but invisible powers, both God's and Satan's, are involved in the larger world scene.

Isn't it good to know that God cannot be successfully opposed? He sets up and puts down even earth's powerful rulers. Have you ever prayed for God's angelic intervention over those who practice evil and the removal of those opposing the spread of the gospel?

Just as Nebuchadnezzar prayed after he was restored to his senses, so would I pray. Lord God, I praise, exalt, and honor You as the King of heaven, for all Your works are true and Your ways just, and You are able to humble those who walk in pride. I pray that, according to Your wise choice, You would remove those from power who oppose the spread of the gospel and the well-being of Your people. May rulers submit to You that we might live a godly and peaceable life and share without restraint Your Word in this dark world. In Jesus' name, amen.

Names of Angelic Ranks

*For by Him [Christ] all things were created, both
in the heavens and on earth, visible and invisible,
whether thrones or dominions or rulers or authorities
—all things have been created through Him and for
Him.* (Colossians 1:16)

God's orderly creation, first described in Genesis 1,
can also be seen in the ranks of angels. The Bible
indicates that there are distinct and graded ranks,
much as in a military organization. Remember that
God is called "the Lord of hosts," the head of armies
of angels. The names *Hosts, Chariots,* and *Watchers*
mentioned earlier suggest this hierarchy. Whether
they are God's obedient angels or angels who serve
Satan, all angels have created or assigned ranks.
The names of these ranks supply us with more
names of angels.

Angels are *ranked by names of class.* The classes
seem to be larger categories with their basic nature
or composition differing in some details from class
to class. *Cherubim* (see chapter 4) seem to hold the
highest position due to their association with God's
presence and glory. Michael, the leader of God's
armies, is probably of the cherub class. However, so
is Satan, who may have been the highest at one
time. He is described in Ezekiel as "the sum, full of
wisdom, and perfect in beauty." He was appointed
to be "the anointed cherub who covers." He was the
head of God's honor guard (Ezekiel 28:12, 14). Not
satisfied with his appointed rank, Satan (then
called Lucifer) coveted advancement—even above
God Himself. He broke God's order and peace and
now promotes disorder and chaos in the human
scene.

We are not certain as to how *seraphim* and the *Living Creatures* (Revelation 4, 5) fit into the organization of ranks, but they obviously are quite highly placed. Perhaps they operated in a "staff position" as worshipers and directors. Both are discussed more fully in chapter 4.

Angels are also *ranked by titles*. Certain names or titles speak of rank. *Archangel* means first among angels, since *arche* means "first" in Greek. Michael alone is called this in the Bible (Jude 9). He is, however, called "one of the chief princes" (Daniel 10:13). Evidently there are other angels of high rank; but probably there is not another archangel, otherwise "first" loses its emphasis.

There are other names of ranks of angels. The order of listing implies military-type organization that is fixed by God's creation. Good angels function by their ranking in God's army. Evil angels, or demons, function by retaining their rank even after their rebellion.

It seems that the descending order of ranks follows this sequence: (1) thrones, (2) dominions, (3) principalities, (4) powers, (5) mights, (6) spiritual wickedness (wicked spirits). Such is the listing in the King James Version. The New American Standard Bible lists (1) thrones, (2) dominions, (3) rulers, (4) authorities, (5) powers, (6) spiritual forces of wickedness.

The name "rulers of the darkness of this world" (Ephesians 6:12 KJV), or "world forces of this darkness" (NASB), refers to those who rule certain areas of the world under the authority of Satan. The Greek term *kosmokratoras* pictures the world in its various facets—political, religious, economic,

cultural—as held down under the power of demonic world rulers, such as we note in Daniel 10,
where we read of "the prince of Persia" and "the
prince of Greece." This term may not reflect rank so
much as function. However, it may be that such
important positions require the high rank named
"thrones."

It is comforting to know that God, in orderly
fashion, rules the world—even the spirit world. Or-
ganized under His assignment and governed by His
wisdom and power, angels carry on their activities
in the human and spirit world, mostly unseen. God
always has the right spiritual forces at the right
place and in the right time. And they delight to follow their Commander in Chief.

God still wants peace and order in His creation
and particularly in His family. Paul ordered the
prophets and the tongues speakers in the early
church, when these gifts were still operative, to limit
their number to two or three at the most. They were
to do this one at a time and each in turn (1 Corinthians
14:26–27). If there was no interpreter, the tongues
speaker was to keep silent (14:28). A similar rule of
order applied to the prophets (14:29–31). All
things were to be done for the edifying of the assembled body (14:26). Paul concludes, "But let all
things be done properly and in an orderly manner"
(14:40).

May our personal and assembly life reflect the
God of peace, not of confusion (14:33). And, by the
way, let us remember that well-organized angels
observe our corporate worship and individual be-
havior (11:10).

Lord Jesus, when I think of Your great wisdom and power in creating the material world and the spiritual world with all its complexities, I am glad that You have the power and wisdom to care for my life and the lives of Your people. May my life reflect Your order and peace in all my relationships and activities, and let Your angels minister to me in the power and wisdom You granted them. Amen.

Chapter 3

MORE NAMES
OF GOOD ANGELS

Angels or demons are not the spirits of deceased humans, as many oriental religions teach; nor are they advanced beings from other planets trying to teach us the path of high learning, life, and power. Advocates of New Age teachings often mistakenly regard angels as part of the natural power structure and energy of the universe, whom we may tap to lead us into full realization and use of our "innate powers."

Instead, God's angels are created spirit beings (Colossians 1:15–16), as we have seen. In addition, they exist to reflect God's character. They are strong and loyal to God, having supernatural power and wisdom given by Him. Several names of angels reflect these qualities:

- Angels of Light
- Sons of the Mighty
- Gods (*Elohim*)
- Sons of God
- Holy Ones
- Stars

Angels of Light

> *For such men are false apostles, deceitful workers,*
> *disguising themselves as apostles of Christ. No wonder,*
> *for even Satan disguises himself as an angel of light.*
> *Therefore it is not surprising if his servants also dis-*
> *guise themselves as servants of righteousness, whose*
> *end will be according to their deeds.* (2 Corinthians
> 11:13–15)

New Age proponents often consider angels as part
of the energy of the universe, whom may be used to
tap into our "innate powers." Clearly, however,
good angels are completely obedient to God and
never deceive humans, as do the spirits contacted
through mediums (channelers). The "spirit guides"
of those involved in the New Age or the occult are
really deceptive demons posing as "angels of light."
Many have been duped, because they have not understood what the Bible teaches.

The name *Angel of Light* appears only in 2 Corinthians 11 in contrast to Satan's servants, both
human and angelic. God's angels are true to God
and reflect His character, which is light, according
to the apostle John. God is light, dwells in light,
and in Him there is no darkness at all (1 John
1:5–7). This means God is truth and holiness, and
He defines what these are. There is no lie or deception in God.

What a contrast to the gods of the pagan soci-
eties surrounding God's people in Bible times and
now! We can trust God to be faithful and true (Ti-
tus 1:2), and He has underwritten His Word with
His name (Psalm 138:2).

God created all angels in light. They had provisional holiness. Some defected with Satan, because

they were not infinitely and unalterably holy. But those to whom God gave grace remained true to Him. The "chosen angels" were confirmed in holiness and light (1 Timothy 5:21). Because of this they are called "Angels of Light." They worship the Lord Jesus and encourage us to do the same, since we are fellow servants with them (Revelation 22:8–9).

Some people may be drawn astray by certain philosophical and secret religions to worship or seek angels as guides to God, but the Bible strictly warns against such (Colossians 2:18–19). Fallen angels have for centuries been leading people to worship false gods (Psalm 106:34–39; 1 Corinthians 10:19–20). Angels of Light would never do that. They encourage us to believe and propagate the gospel of Christ, the Light of the World (Acts 8:26–28; 27:23–24).

Dear Father of light, thank You for sending Your Son to give us the light of salvation. He is the only way, the truth, and the life. My trust is in Him. Keep me from listening to false messages, and lead me in the paths of truth for Your name's sake. Help me to realize what a battle rages for the minds of men and women. Move me to pray against the lie and for the truth. In Jesus' name, amen.

Sons of the Mighty

Ascribe to the Lord, O sons of the mighty, ascribe to the Lord glory and strength. Ascribe to the Lord the glory due his name; worship the Lord in holy array. (Psalm 29:1–2)

Psalm 29:1 and Psalm 89:6 call angels *bene elim*. This Hebrew expression describes the great strength of angels (cf. Psalm 103:20). In the Hebrew language, the term "son(s) of" refers to a class of persons. The prophets were called "sons of the prophets," not in a genetic sense, but in the sense that they belonged to a group of official messengers of God. Some difficult or lawless person would be called a "son of Belial," meaning a worthless fellow (1 Samuel 2:12; 25:17, 25). Jesus called James and John "sons of thunder" because of their noisy and damaging thoughts.

Since *Elim* refers to the multiplication of strength, or the greatness of strength, *Sons of the Mighty* describes angels as a class of strong ones who carry out the will of the God who gives them strength.

Yes, God has an innumerable company of angels, strong and loyal. They care for His own. As Sons of the Mighty, they may intervene on our behalf at times either known or unknown to us.

You, my heavenly Father, are the source of all strength. Ultimate power belongs to You. Thank You for creating and appointing strong angels to praise You and to protect Your people. Continue Your care of me and my loved ones and friends, and send Your strong angels to protect my way. In Jesus' name, amen.

Gods (Elohim)

What is man, that You are mindful of him, and the son of man that You visit him? For You have made him a little lower than the angels, and You have crowned him with glory and honor. (Psalm 8:4–5 NKJV)

Elohim is the general name for God, as in Genesis 1, the creation story. He is the Strong One who created all in heaven and earth, in fact, the whole universe. However, the same term is also used of false gods (Exodus 20:3; Isaiah 37:12; Jeremiah 22:9), of angels (Genesis 35:7, Hebrew, plural verb), of demons (Psalm 97:7), and even of men who acted as God's representatives (Psalm 82:6). The Hebrews who translated the Hebrew Old Testament into Greek to give us the Septuagint (about 250 to 150 B.C.), used the term *angelos* in Psalm 8:5. Actually, the text says that God made mankind "a little lower than God (*elohim*)." The writer of Hebrews could use, under the inspiration of the Holy Spirit, the Septuagint translation in Hebrews 2:9, where he speaks of Christ being made "a little lower than angels (*angelos*)," or genuine human, for the suffering of death in the place of humans so that He might secure our forgiveness.

This term pictures the angels belonging to a class of beings, including God (though not equal with God), who are strong and cannot die, as do humans. They have great strength and powers above weak and mortal man. Moses described Jacob's encounter at Bethel as a revelation of angels (*elohim* with a plural verb).

As created beings, angels reflect God's great power and enjoy endless life. They are stronger than we are, but they delight to serve God and us with all their strength. We are weak and mortal; but one day, when the Lord raises His own from the dead and transforms the living (1 Corinthians 15:51–54), we shall be as angels, never dying again and never needing to replenish a dying race (Matthew 22:29–32). Even now, however, those who have trusted Christ have been legally crucified, raised, and seated with Christ in the heavenlies far above the position of angels (Romans 6:3; Ephesians 1:19–2:6).

Because the Holy Spirit has baptized believers into Christ, we share a position with Christ that angels can never enjoy. We can marvel at such power and such grace and give our God and Savior unending praise.

Heavenly Father, I recognize that I am weak, beset with human limitations and subject to death. But I thank You for creating us as valuable persons, made in Your image. Thank You for highly esteeming us and for visiting us in the person of Your Son to redeem us and raise us far above angels. I marvel at Your grace and Your power to raise Jesus and us from the dead and exalting Him and us to Your right hand, seated in the heavenlies. Let me keep this in mind as I seek to walk in victory over sin and Satan. In Jesus' name, amen.

Sons of God

Now there was a day when the sons of God came
to present themselves before the LORD, *and Satan also*
came among them. (Job 1:6)

The term *sons of God,* translated from the Hebrew
bene elohim, refers to angels as a class of mighty
ones or powers. It is used of angels in Job 1:6; 2:1;
38:7. The prologue to Job's story (chapters 1–2)
was probably written after the whole scenario of
suffering to enlighten Job and us as to what was going on behind the scenes. Job probably didn't know
(as we know from Job 1:6) that Satan was involved.
But when God called all the *sons of God* to appear
before Him, Satan was among them. He also must
obey God when He speaks. Satan stood among a
class of beings called *elohim.* This latter term is the
name used of God, but it is also used of false gods
and demons, as we noted earlier.

It is obvious, then, that *sons of God* does not refer to their holy nature but to them as a class of
mighty ones who, like God, never die. This name
contrasts angels with men who do die. Angels are
immortal. They have no physical body to die. Once
created, they never cease to exist. Good angels live
with God forever, but evil angels will spend eternity
with Satan in the Lake of Fire (Hebrews 12:25;
Matthew 25:41).

Some say that this term is also used of God's
own people; but close inspection of the passages
usually listed (Deuteronomy 14:1; Hosea 1:10;
11:1) will show that the exact term is not used.
Bene elohim is a technical term for angels and is
probably the sense in which "the sons of God" in
Genesis 6 is used.

But God uses the activities of these sons of God for His own glory. In Job 1–2, Satan had slandered Job and God. Job served God only as long as God kept him and blessed him, Satan claimed. God used Satan's evil desires in afflicting Job to vindicate His own character and to educate Job. Job learned that the better part of wisdom is to trust God implicitly, even when he didn't understand what was happening.

When we do not understand and wonder whether God hears or cares, we can trust Him. God *does* care and has good plans for us. They may not appear soon or even in this life; but if God is for us—and He certainly is—then no one, man or angel, can be against us (Romans 8:31–39). Even Job's outcome showed that "the Lord is full of compassion and is merciful" (James 5:11).

Thank You, Lord God, that You care for me, protect me, and send Your angels to guard me. I'm so glad that You limit the plans and activities of Satan and demons. That truth comforts and encourages me. I could never survive the onslaught of evil without Your specific intervention. Help me to trust You in times of distress, even though I don't know the whys. May I not forget that You are gracious and merciful. In Jesus' name, amen.

Holy Ones

*Behold, the Lord came with many thousands of
His holy ones, to execute judgment upon all, and to
convict all the ungodly of all their ungodly deeds which
they have done in an ungodly way, and of all the harsh
things which ungodly sinners have spoken against Him.*
(Jude 14b–15)

"For who in the skies is comparable to the Lord?"
asked the psalmist. "Who among the sons of the
mighty is like the Lord, a God greatly feared in the
council of the holy ones, and awesome above all
those who are around Him" (Psalm 89:6–7). Here
Ethan used parallel statements, a common device
of Hebrew poetry, to equate "sons of the mighty"
with "the holy ones." The Hebrew word is *ka-
doshim,* which means "separated ones; those set
apart to God." This should be understood as referring to angels. We find the same expression in Job
5:1; 15:15; Daniel 8:13; and Zechariah 14:5. In
each case, it seems to refer to angels.

This term reflects their holy character and activities as devoted to God. The New Testament
book of Jude quotes the book of Enoch with ap-
proval and notes: "Behold, the Lord came with
many thousands of His holy ones (verse 14)." Here
the Greek *hagiais* reflects the Hebrew use of "holy
ones."

Angels are ones set apart to God by His creation and by their dedication. They are "holy ones"
in that sense. We who are in Christ are holy ones,
or saints. We are set apart to God by creation, by
recreation in Christ (Ephesians 4:24), and can be
His by dedication.

How futile life would be if we did not recognize that God has redeemed us—something He has not done and cannot do for angels—and wants us to give our lives completely over to Him for His development and use. Angels delight to be His and His alone. Why shouldn't we?

Father in heaven, I recognize that You have set angels apart for Your fellowship and service. They must enjoy such grace! I relish the truth that You have set me apart for Yourself by purchasing me back from guilt and a false lifestyle and by granting me the Holy Spirit to enable me to fellowship with You. Through the Spirit I can serve You acceptably until Jesus comes again. I give myself to You for Your plans for me. Amen.

Stars

Where were you when I laid the foundation of the earth? Tell Me, if you have understanding. . . . When the morning stars sang together and all the sons of God shouted for joy? (Job 38:4, 7)

Stars are heavenly bodies. As such they are a fitting symbol for angelic heavenly beings. God challenged Job, asking him as to where he was when God created all the world and "the morning stars sang together and all the sons of God *(bene elohim)* shouted for joy" (Job 38:7). Both stars and angels reflect the power and wisdom of God. They are often mentioned in the same context (cf. Psalm 148:1–5).

The host of heaven in the Old Testament refers to both physical stars and angels (Deuteronomy 4:19; 17:3; 1 Kings 22:19; Nehemiah 9:6; Psalm 33:6). The term connects the worship of heavenly bodies with worship of demons, who are evil angels. Reforming King Josiah "did away with the idolatrous priests . . . also those who burned incense to Baal, to the sun and to the moon and to the constellations and to all the host of heaven" (2 Kings 23:5). Fortune-telling and the worship of stars is condemned by God (Deuteronomy 18:10–14) as connected to demons. Even Satan is described in Revelation 12:3–4 as a "sign in heaven . . . a great red dragon . . . and his tail swept away a third of the stars of heaven, and threw them to the earth." These are later described as "Satan . . . and his angels" (verse 9).

The term *stars,* then, speaks symbolically of heavenly spirits created by God. The star-filled heavens and the angelic ranks both have their own beauty. We can see the starry host of heaven, but the spiritual host of heaven belong to the unseen world, both good and evil.

We need to ask God for alertness to the reality of the spirit world and to discern evil spirits. Certainly we should avoid any form of astrology, a religion begun in Babylon and Egypt. God required severe judgment upon those who "served other gods and worshiped them, or the sun or the moon or any of the heavenly host" (Deuteronomy 17:3).

Perhaps as we view the stars at night, we might thank Him for His creative genius. We could also thank Him for the hosts of heaven who protect His people, and we could pray against the hosts of the enemy who would oppose His person, His program, and His people.

Thank You, my heavenly Father, that You rule heaven and earth. You made them. You govern them. Because You are strong, they continue in their positions. Thank You that You also support Your chosen angels. They marveled at Your creating the heavens and the earth. They know that heavenly bodies do not govern our lives. I know that You are the governor of my life. I trust You to lead me and to provide all the wisdom and power I need to live in this world. I will not seek forbidden knowledge. I ask You to defeat the forces of darkness that oppose You and Your people and to make us aware of the enemy's tactics. In Jesus' name, amen.

Chapter 4

NAMES OF
HIGH RANKING ANGELS

Cherubim and seraphim falling down before
Thee,
Which wert and art, and evermore shalt be."

The words of *Holy, Holy, Holy,* one of the church's
mighty hymns, describe two classes of angels pros-
trate before a holy God. The cherubim and seraphim do honor God's holiness, among their duties.
In addition, the Living Creatures of Revelation 4
and 5 constantly worship God. In this chapter we
will meet those special groups of angels:

- The Cherubim
- The Seraphim
- The Living Creatures

The Cherubim:
Their Description

> *And the cherubim appeared to have the form of a man's hand under their wings . . . And each one had four faces. . . . Then the cherubim rose up. They are the living beings that I saw by the river Chebar.* (Ezekiel 10:8, 14, 15)

In the mysterious, supernatural world, there are many types of angels. They are not all created equal. They have no problem with that. They are glad to be alive and to be able to serve the true and living God, the Most High. They are all genuine persons, but they differ in their characteristics and their assigned positions, powers, and duties. God has placed each just where He wants him.

Cherubim (Hebrew plural of *cherub*) seem to be the highest class of angelic beings. They seem to be sent as messengers, and the name *angel* means "messenger." The cherubim were created with indescribable beauty and powers. Their real character and appearance in the spirit world is far beyond human comprehension, so they are described for us in terms that humans can begin to understand (Ezekiel 1:5–14; 28:12–13, 17).

Depending upon what would best serve the occasion for which they are sent or pictured, God caused them to appear in various forms. They first appeared on earth after Adam and Eve violated the command of God and sinned. God "drove the man out; and at the east of the Garden of Eden He stationed the cherubim, and the flaming sword which turned every direction, to guard the way to the tree of life" (Genesis 3:24). He did this, we understand, lest sinful humans should intrude into God's presence or presume to partake of the tree of life to live forever. Cherubim teach us that sin and paradise are not compatible. Sinners cannot approach a holy God without the removal of guilt and the sentence of death and without the righteousness graciously granted to those who trust the Savior, the Lord Jesus.

Cherubim came on the biblical scene next in the tabernacle used in the Mosaic Law system. They appeared in the form of golden images standing on the mercy seat, the lid of the Ark of the Covenant inside the most holy place, a representation of God's presence (Exodus 25:17–22). There, sometimes, the Shechinah glory of God rested. They were also atop the mercy seat in Solomon's temple (2 Chronicles 3:10–13). In this connection, they are called "the cherubim of glory" (Hebrews 9:5), being closely associated with the manifest glory of God. They also appeared embroidered on the veil that closed off the most holy place, later on the walls of Solomon's temple, and in Ezekiel's vision of the new temple during Messiah's kingdom reign (Ezekiel 41). Again, they were associated with God's holiness, guarding the way to God.

When Ezekiel was taken to Babylon, due to the capture of Jerusalem, God gave him a vision of the glory of God. And who should be associated with God's glorious presence, but the cherubim! They are called "four living creatures" (Ezekiel 1:1–28), later identified as cherubim (10:4, 18–22).

The cherubim were not described in Genesis 3, but Ezekiel pictured them as complicated, intricate, unusual creatures. Each one had four faces and four wings, and the overall appearance could be likened to a man (1:5–6), not like the mythical Egyptian sphinx or winged lion. They had hands of a man under their wings (1:8). The four faces of each of them were likened to a man, a lion, a bull, and an eagle (1:10). They glistened as polished bronze and bright coals of fire, and their movements flashed as lightning (10:7, 13–14).

They would have been an awesome sight to have beheld, as they reflected their duties to an awesome, holy God.

Lord God of Hosts, I cannot begin to understand the marvels of Your creations here on earth, let alone the intricacies of Your designs in the spirit world. I marvel at the awesomeness of the cherubim. I marvel more at Your glory and holiness. How could I ever approach You except Your having provided for me, through faith, the righteousness of Christ? Thank You that I may come boldly before Your throne with confidence and joy. Amen.

The Cherubim:
Their Design and Duties

The Lord reigns, let the peoples tremble; He is enthroned above the cherubim, let the earth shake!
(Psalm 99:1)

For what purpose did God create *cherubim* and to what activities does He assign them? They are *proclaimers and protectors of God's glorious presence, sovereignty, and holiness.* They mark God's presence, as in the Garden of Eden, the most holy place in the tabernacle and later the temple. Psalms 80:1 and 99:1 refer to the Shechinah glory as representing God who is "enthroned above the cherubim."

They also *proclaim to men the transcendent and unapproachable God,* since they forbid entrance to paradise and guard His presence in the tabernacle. From the vision in Ezekiel 1, they *picture the intervention of a sovereign God in the affairs of the human race.* They are positioned in this vision under the four corners of a ruler's dais, or platform, on which the glory of God was seated in the appearance of a man upon His throne (1:22–23, 26). Under each cherub were two wheels, of the same size, concentric and at right angles, centered on the same vertical axis. These wheels, then, could run in any direction without needing a turning radius or time to turn. The throne was propelled by the powerful wings of the cherubim with a great rushing noise (1:9, 24). The whole vision portrayed the glory of God moving swiftly and sovereignly upon the earth and in heaven to accomplish His holy purposes and judgments.

Surveying the book of Ezekiel, we see the glory of God associated with the cherubim, as God judges the sin of Israel and of the nations and intervenes for Israel to accomplish His promised ultimate blessing upon His chosen people in the messianic kingdom.

Significantly, the cherubim upon the mercy seat look downward to see the blood sprinkled on the lid of the ark to cover the sins of the people. Inside the ark are the reminders of God's gracious provisions that the Israelites had rejected: the pot of manna, the tables of Law, and Aaron's budded rod. So cherubim, proclaimers and protectors of God's holiness, symbolically see the sins of the people covered by a satisfying sacrifice.

How wonderful the picture of Christ's sacrifice that propitiated God's holiness and Law! His blood, His whole personal sacrifice, satisfies God completely and allows us to approach a holy God through our Great High Priest and to dwell in His presence permanently. Cherubim are *proclaimers of the grace of God* that provides sinners access and assurance of eternal life.

Wonderful Triune God—Father, Son, and Holy Spirit—I worship You in Your indescribable beauty of holiness. I marvel that You who demonstrated Your presence above the cherubim have made me Your innermost sanctuary. Let me guard Your temple, my body, from defilement, and sanctify it to Your use. Demonstrate Your glory in me through Your Spirit. In Jesus' name, amen.

The Seraphim:
Their Description

Seraphim stood above Him, each having six wings; with two he covered his face, and with two he covered his feet, and with two he flew. And one called out to another and said, "Holy, Holy, Holy, is the Lord of Hosts, the whole earth is full of His glory." (Isaiah 6:2–3)

The *seraphim* (Hebrew plural of *seraph*) are another special class of angels associated with the glory and holiness of God. They are mentioned only in Isaiah 6. The Hebrew word means "burning ones." Inwardly they are consumed with devotion to God and praise Him perfectly. They are presented in somewhat human form with faces, hands, and feet.

But they also have six wings. What do the three sets of wings depict? The two that cover their faces tell us that even the most high and perfect creatures cannot bear the unguarded sight of God's glory. Another set of wings covering their feet symbolize their reverence and hesitancy to tread uninvited into God's presence. The third set of wings allows them to swiftly do God's will.

In Isaiah 6, several seraphim hovered above and on both sides of Jehovah *(Yahweh)* upon His throne. They cried back and forth, as antiphonal choirs, "Holy, Holy, Holy is the Lord of Hosts; the whole earth is full of His glory." The thrice repeated "holy," in Hebrew idiom, means "extremely holy." The force of their voices shook the supports of the throne room (verse 4). The altar probably speaks of the golden altar of incense that stood before the veil that shut off the most holy place from the rest of the tabernacle. Only the high priest, once a year, and not without blood, entered the most holy place with smoke from the incense, signifying that sinful man could not look directly upon the holiness of God. Isaiah's temple in the vision was filled with smoke (verse 4).

Again, holy Father, I stand in awe at Your infinite and perfect holiness. Not even sinless, marvelous seraphim can bear to gaze upon You. But You have invited me to come without hesitation to Your throne of grace. I come because I am weak and needy. Though I am perfectly accepted in Your beloved Son, yet I still fight sinful inclinations and motivations within. Thank You for Your Holy Spirit who can push sin off the throne of my life and enables me to walk in holiness in Jesus. Amen.

The Seraphim:
Their Design and Duties

> *Then one of the seraphim flew to me with a burning coal in his hand, which he had taken from the altar with tongs. He touched my mouth with it and said, "Behold, this has touched your lips; and your iniquity is taken away and your sin is forgiven."* (Isaiah 6:6–7)

Only God-appointed humans could be priests under the old covenant Law. No man took this honor to himself (Hebrews 5:1–10). Even Christ, the God-man, was appointed by God—not by birthright in Levi's line, but by an oath-right that established Him as a priest forever after the order of Melchizedek. In their priestly type of service for God, the seraphim did not represent angels or men with sacrifice and intercession, however. Instead, they ministered in His presence to *praise and proclaim God's perfect holiness.* They also *proclaimed that man must be cleansed* of sin's defilement that he might stand before God and serve Him.

One of them, upon Isaiah's confession of his innate sinfulness, flew with a live coal from the altar and touched Isaiah's lips to purge his sin (6:6–7). This symbolizes the real cleansing that God gives his children upon confession of sin (1 John 1:9). Once cleansed, we are ready to speak God's message to men (6:8–9).

Isaiah's sin was not the misuse of his mouth. The cleansing of his unclean lips is reminiscent of the patch on the lip of the leper and his cry of "unclean, unclean" (Leviticus 13:45). Leprosy speaks of inner disease breaking out, just as our sinful nature does. In the context, Isaiah mentions the death of King Uzziah, who was struck with leprosy for intruding into God's presence (2 Chronicles 26:16–21).

We are guilty for the very nature we have, from which stems all outward sin. It is our basic sin (Romans 7:14–25). It is for the cleansing and defeat of this sin also that Christ died (Romans 8:1–4). If we say we don't have the guilt of such sin, then "we are deceiving ourselves, and the truth is not in us" (1 John 1:8). But we need not bemoan our innate sinfulness. We need to recognize it as present and powerful, but thank God for its defeat by our co-crucifixion with Christ (Romans 6:6). Now we must confess our sin and yield to the Holy Spirit who will lead us in victory over sin (Romans 8:4; Galatians 5:16–18) and produce within us the holy fruit of the Spirit (Galatians 5:22–23). God Himself and the cherubim would be pleased with that response.

Lord Jesus, my great High Priest, I thank You for Your sacrifice and intercession on my behalf. Thank You for dying to cancel the guilt of my sinful nature as well as my sinful acts. Bring to my mind what sins might prevent me from the enjoyment of Your fellowship and from serving You fully. Your seraphim remind me of Your demands for holiness and of Your cleansing through Your blood shed for me. Here am I. Use me. Amen.

The Living Creatures:
Their Identity

And before the throne there was, something like, a sea of glass like crystal; and in the center and around the throne, four living creatures full of eyes in front and behind. (Revelation 4:6)

When you really want to know what a person is thinking, you watch his eyes. Athletes looking for an edge in football, wrestling, and boxing sometimes gaze into their opponents' eyes. Even in everyday conversations, we watch the other person's eyes, for they often reveal thoughts or feelings. Eyes even reflect intelligence. We might say, "The eyes have it!"

The four living creatures of Revelation 4:6 are described as being "full of eyes in front and behind." In these living creatures we encounter perhaps the most intelligent and complex spirit beings in God's universe. They may not be properly called angels, because they seem never to serve as messengers to men. However, they do deliver messages to angels. We see four *living beings* (Greek, *zoa*) standing at the four corners of the dais where God sits on His throne in the heavenly scene of Revelation 4 and 5. Who are these unusual creatures?

They remind us of the living creatures of Ezekiel 1. Are they, then, cherubim? There is reference to faces like a lion, a calf, a man, and an eagle, and to multiple wings and to many eyes. However, there are striking differences. Here in Revelation, each has only one face, whereas in Ezekiel each had four faces. In Revelation, each has six wings; in Ezekiel, they had four. In Revelation, they have eyes around and within; in Ezekiel, the eyes were in the wheels, and the spirits of the cherubim were in the wheels. In Revelation, they do not move; in Ezekiel, they propelled the throne of the sovereign God throughout the world.

Some think that they are seraphim, who also have six wings and cry, "Holy, Holy, Holy" (Isaiah

6:1–3; Revelation 4:8). We cannot be certain of their identity, but the eyes within and around seem to speak of their extreme intelligence.

Lord God Almighty, as I further explore through Your Scriptures the marvels of the spirit world, I am utterly taken back, speechless, as I consider the unimaginable power and intelligence of the creatures You have made. Yet I must marvel much more at the greatness and majesty of Your person. There is none like You. Even Your highest creatures confess that and praise You. Increase my understanding of Your person and appreciation of Your omnipotence and omniscience. I worship You for who You are and for Your grace and love for me. Amen.

The Living Creatures:
Their Activities

And the four living creatures, each one of them having six wings, are full of eyes around and within; and day and night they do not cease to say, "Holy, Holy, Holy, is the Lord God, The Almighty, who was and who is and who is to come." (Revelation 4:8)

What do these extremely intelligent and specially positioned creatures do? Revelation 4:8 describes their unending, uninterrupted worship of the Living God, who is *Yahweh,* the Almighty, the self-existent and unchanging God. So "the living creatures give glory and honor and thanks to Him who sits on the throne, to Him who lives forever and ever." Thus we see them worshiping and praising God in chapters 4, 5, 7, and 19. They witness the worship of redeemed humans in Revelation 14.

They also will be directing the judgments of God during the Great Tribulation, that last seven-year period that Daniel predicted for Israel and the Gentiles. In Revelation 6, they each in turn called for the execution of the judgments of the first four seals of the scroll; and in Revelation 15, one of them gave to seven other angels the seven bowls of the wrath of God to be poured out upon the earth. If we understand that the cleansing of Isaiah by fire and the punishment of the earth by judgment are both expressions of purging by a holy God, then we may have an additional reason for thinking that the living creatures are seraphim.

If these extremely intelligent beings, who understand more than we can of the mystery and majesty of the true and living God, give unceasing honor and praise to God, ought not we give what strength we have to honoring and praising this One who is our Father in heaven?

These *living creatures* never question as they carry out vast judgments for the holy and righteous God they serve. What place is there for sin-twisted, creaturely minds to question the right of God to judge all evil and unrepentant sinners? If God cannot judge the world in righteousness, what right does He have to be God? But when God does judge the world's false and idolatrous politico-religious system, these great spirit beings cry, "Hallelujah! Salvation and glory and power belong to our God; because His judgments are true and righteous; for He has judged the great harlot who was corrupting the earth with her immorality, and He has avenged the blood of His bond-servants on her" (Revelation 19:1b–2).

Let us also bow in worship of God's extreme holiness and trust Him to judge righteously at the proper time and in the proper way. He is the Lord God Almighty. We honor Him and His Son to whom all judgment is given (John 5:22).

O righteous Father, I bow before You in adoration and praise. You and You alone are God, and You alone have the right to sit upon the throne of the universe. You have the right to judge. You have given all judgment to Your Son, Jesus, the God-man. I repent of any questioning of Your ways or Your right to judge the world. You judged my sin in the sacrifice of Your Son. I can trust You to do what is right in my life. Let me use all my heart, soul, strength, and mind to love You in Spirit and in truth. Amen.

Chapter 5

THREE
MIGHTY ANGELS

Some may think it strange, but just two of God's angels have personal names revealed in the Bible: Michael and Gabriel. God has given each of them an important place among angels, and each is mentioned in the Old and New Testaments four times. Michael seems to be the military leader, while Gabriel is a leading messenger. A third angel, though not given a specific personal name, seems to be a theophany, an appearance of God upon the earth.

In this chapter we will wonder at the power and help of these mighty angels:

- Michael
- Gabriel
- The Angel of Jehovah

Michael

*And there was war in heaven, Michael and his
angels waging war with the dragon. The dragon and
his angels waged war, and they were not strong enough,
and there was no longer a place found for them in
heaven. And the great dragon was thrown down.*
(Revelation 12:7–9a)

When I have met men with the name Michael, I often
have asked them if they knew what their name meant.
Did they know it was Hebrew and an outstanding
name? Most have never thought of the answer, and
some thought it was a Christian name. Then I explained to them the meaning and significance of
the name. It sometimes lays a foundation for further witness to the Bible and to the Lord Jesus.

Along with many, I understand the name *Michael*
to form a question: "Who is like God?" It is com-
posed of three parts: *mi*, meaning "who"; *ci*, meaning
"like"; and *el*, the name for God, emphasizing power.
This is a humble assertion that there is no one who
could ever compare to our Creator God. Michael is
humble, completely devoted to God and to doing
His will. What a stark contrast to Satan's proud and
selfish assertion, "I will make myself like [God]."
(Isaiah 14:14).

There are those who take the name to be an assertion, declaring that its bearer is God: "Who is like
me, who am God!" It seems later Jewish scholars
identified Michael with the Shechinah. The Jehovah Witnesses, who say that Christ was the first
created being, a lesser god, identify Michael as the
appearance of the preincarnate Christ. Neverthe-
less, it seems quite clear in the Bible that Michael is
a created angel and not God. Men assumed that

name often, from Numbers 13:13 to Ezra 8:8. We note that Michael is an archangel and "one of the chief princes" (Daniel 10:13), as if he belongs to a class of high ranking angels. He has assignments, much as do other angels, over the political world scene. In contrast, Christ is stated to be genuine and complete deity (John 1:1; Colossians 2:9). Christ is unique (Greek, *monogenes*, "one of a kind"), created all angels (Colossians 1:16), and is the Lord of all nations (Revelation 19:13–16).

Michael is "the archangel" (Jude 9). There are no other archangels mentioned in the Bible, although some Jewish scholars hold that there are seven. This title sets Michael above most of the angels. He is the military leader of any army of God's angels. In the Great Tribulation, this army will do battle with Satan's angels (Revelation 12:7). While the definite article in the expression "the archangel" does not necessarily limit the class to Michael, it does point out a well-known archangel. There might be others of the same class, since Michael is mentioned as "one of the chief princes" (Daniel 13:10). Perhaps he is first (Greek, *arche*) among the chief angelic rulers, something like the chief of staff among the ranking generals in the U.S. Pentagon. He may also be one of the cherubim class, as is Satan with whom he wages war (Ezekiel 28:14–18; Revelation 12:7).

Among his duties, Michael is the *military leader of God's army of angels*. In addition, God has also granted him the position of *guardian of God's chosen nation, Israel* to protect its people and to oppose their enemies.

In Daniel's time, an angel of lower rank and power than Michael was sent from heaven to Daniel to answer his prayers and to give revelation regarding Israel's future and the end times. However, he was delayed in transit three weeks by an opposing spirit ruler, a demon, called "the prince of Persia." Then came Michael, the angel said, "to help me, for I had been left there with the kings of Persia" (Daniel 10:13). After the angel delivered God's message to Daniel, he left to do battle in the spirit world with "the prince of Greece. . . . Yet there is no one who stands firmly with me against these *forces* except Michael your prince" (10:20–21).

What amazing insight God has given us that we should understand what goes on behind the human scene in the spirit world! Elect angels wrestling with evil angels for influence and control of world political powers is something that the leaders and politicians of few countries understand. We can certainly pray against both human and supernatural forces that oppose Christ's purpose to spread the gospel and build His church. He said to Peter and His disciples, "I will build my church, and the gates [authorities] of Hades [the unseen world of spirits] shall not overpower it."

One specific assignment given to Michael is to be "the great prince who stands guard over the sons of your people" (Daniel's people, Israel). This will take on great importance during the coming Great Tribulation, the "time of Jacob's distress" (Jeremiah 30:7). We can see this action in Daniel 12:1: "Now at that time Michael, the great prince who stands *guard* over the sons of your people, will arise. And there will be a time of distress such as never occurred since there was a nation until that time; and at that time your people, everyone who is found written in the book, will be rescued" (italics added).

This is the unprecedented, unparalleled tribulation that the Lord Jesus said would immediately precede His return to earth to rescue His people and destroy His enemies (Matthew 24:15–31). At that time Michael will exercise his power to protect God's people against both human and satanic opposition. Under God, Michael and his army of angels will conquer Satan and his angels as part of the total victory won by Christ, the coming King of Kings and Lord of Lords (Revelation 12:10; 19:11–16).

Even though he is great and powerful, Michael respects Satan's power. "Michael the archangel, when he disputed with the devil and argued about the body of Moses, did not dare pronounce against him a railing judgment, but said, 'The Lord rebuke you!'" (Jude 9). He respected the personal dignity of Satan and did not blaspheme him. If one so great as Michael, the head of all God's angelic armies, did not rely on his own strength and mock Satan, how much more must we rely upon God for our stand against Satan and his demonic hordes (Ephesians 6:10–12; 2 Peter 2:11). Our position "in Christ" puts us far above all angels, but we must war with utter dependence upon the Lord and not assume that we have strength in ourselves.

O Lord of Hosts, thank You that You control the affairs of men and angels and have given Your angels charge of world affairs and the matters of my life. Thank You for Your angels who war under Michael,

*their leader, to protect Your chosen people. Help me and
other believers to grasp the larger world scene as angels
and men battle for truth and righteousness. Help me to
battle in the strength of the Lord. Amen.*

Gabriel

*The angel answered and said to him, "I am
Gabriel, who stands in the presence of God, and I have
been sent to speak to you and to bring you this good
news." (Luke 1:19)*

Gabriel is another mighty angel of God. He is a
faithful servant, delivering wonderful messages
about Messiah's kingdom.

The name *Gabriel* means "mighty one of God"
(from two Hebrew words, *gabor,* "mighty one"; and
el, "God"). God created him with great strength.
Gabriel demonstrated this as he flew with unusual
speed to Daniel (Daniel 9:21). He further is described as "the man Gabriel" (9:21), reflecting the
human form of his appearance. He is also "the angel Gabriel" (Luke 1:26), revealing his nature as angelic. He describes himself: "I am Gabriel, who
stands in the presence of God" (Luke 1:19). This
special messenger has permanent access to the
presence of God.

Gabriel often appears in appropriate human
form to present messages to humans. Daniel writes,
"Then this one with human appearance touched
me again and strengthened me" (Daniel 10:18).
Gabriel spoke with a human voice (10:17–20) and
had the power of touch much like a man's (8:18;
10:18). He could stand in one particular location as
he appeared to Zecharias, the father of John the
Baptist, causing him great fear (Luke 1:11–12). When

Mary, the mother of Jesus' humanity, saw him, she didn't seem as much troubled by his appearance as by what he said about her coming supernatural offspring (Luke 1:26–29). This may be due to his friendly appearance and approach.

We understand that Michael is God's special military leader and angelic champion for Israel. But Gabriel is God's special messenger of Messiah's kingdom program. In each of the four times he appears in the scriptural record, He delivers messages concerning the coming Messiah, the Lord Jesus, and His great earthly kingdom. This is the emphasis of his ministry in the Old Testament to Daniel and in the New Testament to Zecharias and Mary.

His most amazing message came to Mary. He gave her the startling news that she would conceive and give birth to a son whose name would be Jesus (Hebrew, *Yeshua*), which means Jehovah (Hebrew, *Yaweh*) saves. He further stated, "He will be great, and will be called the Son of the Most High; and the Lord God will give Him the throne of His father David; and He will reign over the house of Jacob forever; and His kingdom will have no end" (Luke 1:32–33).

When Mary asked how this would come about since she was a virgin, Gabriel revealed that the Holy Spirit would cause the virgin to conceive in her womb; so that her human offspring would be joined to the Son of God (verses 34–35). Never before had this concept been made so clear. The eternal Son, fully God, would add full humanity (without sin), so that He, as the person of the God-man, could reveal God fully while in human form on earth (John 14:9). Further, as God-man He could represent us to God as our Great High Priest and offer himself a spotless, eternal sacrifice to satisfy God's wrath regarding sin and to gain eternal life for all who personally receive Him (Hebrews 2:17; 9:11–15).

The Lord Jesus came the first time to lay the basis for the forgiveness of sins and for justification before God (Romans 5:1). He came, as well, to destroy the works of the devil (1 John 3:8). In accord with Gabriel's message, Christ will come the second time to establish His reign upon David's throne and rule over the whole inhabited world in righteousness (Isaiah 9:6–7).

I suppose that if Gabriel could come to you, he might ask you, along with me, if you have trusted Christ for the great saving work finished on the cross at Christ's first coming. For receiving His Son, God freely—without human works or cost—grants eternal life (John 3:16; Ephesians 2:8–9).

Gabriel might also ask if you are looking with anticipation for Christ's second coming when He will be revealed in His glory and with the holy angels to set up His kingdom and judge His enemies (Matthew 24:31–46). This present world scene is not all that we can expect. We hope for the presence of the Lord Jesus and all the blessings that come with Him. What devoted and godly lives we should live as we, who love the Lord Jesus, eagerly wait for His return (1 John 3:23; 2 Peter 3:9–13).

Thank You, heavenly Father, for the good news that Jesus has come to join the human race and that He is coming again to restore peace and righteousness on the earth. Your angelic messenger Gabriel encouraged

us with Your kingdom message that Jesus shall reign.
May He reign in my heart today and every day until He
comes again, and please make it soon. Amen.

The Angel of Jehovah:
His Identity

And the angel of Jehovah appeared unto him
[Moses] in a flaming fire out of the midst of a bush;
and he looked, and, and, behold, the bush burned with fire,
and the bush was not consumed. (Exodus 3:2 ASV)

Here is an Angel that surpasses all those called
angels. He is more than any type of angel. Some
would say he is God, like the preincarnate Son of
God, the Lord Christ. If this is the case, then the angel is a theophany, an appearance of God in visible
and bodily form. How can we know who this angel
might be? Let's check the evidence.

The Angel of Jehovah (Hebrew, *Malak Yaweh*)
appears in the Old Testament only. He comes on
the scene of the biblical record beginning with the
time of Abraham and extending to the time of
Zechariah. He has no continuous story line, but appears only on special occasions.

Significantly, this angel is identified with Jehovah. While the name *elohim* was used of the true
and living Creator God, it was used also of the gods
of the heathen. But the name *Yahweh* was reserved
for the God who revealed himself to Abraham and
the nation Israel. The name refers to the eternal,
self-existent God who made heaven and earth and
who entered into personal and covenant relationship with His people. Some understand *Yahweh* to
be an imperfect of the Hebrew verb *hayah,* and it
might be translated "I am what I shall be." This God

never changes. His essence and character remain always the same. Malachi 3:6 says, "For I, the Lord *[Yahweh]*, do not change; therefore you, O sons of Jacob, are not consumed."

The Angel of Jehovah has a peculiar title; angels in general are "the sons of God" *(bene elohim)* but never "the sons of Jehovah" *(bene Yahweh)*. Since this angel alone has this title, a peculiar title of *Malak Yahweh,* we might deduce that he is a very special angel, more than an angel, and perhaps Jehovah Himself.

This angel's personal identity is regarded through the scriptural record as equal to Jehovah. His first appearance is to Sarai's slave girl, Hagar. He found Hagar in the wilderness fleeing from harsh treatment from her mistress (Genesis 16:7). He took mercy upon her and promised her things that only God could do (verse 10). Moses, who tells the story, identifies the angel as "Jehovah that spake unto her" (16:13 ASV). When "the angel of Jehovah *[Yahweh]* appeared to him in a flaming fire out of the midst of a bush," (Exodus 3:2; "angel of the Lord" in NASB), he is called "Jehovah" (3:4 ASV). He identified himself: "'I am the God of your father, the God of Abraham, the God of Isaac, and the God of Jacob.' Then Moses hid his face, for he was afraid to look at God" (3:6). This is the occasion when God revealed His name as "I Am Who I Am" and commissioned Moses to go in the name of "I Am" (3:14). God did not entrust the revelation of His covenant and memorial name to a mere angel. He revealed it Himself in the personal appearance of the Angel of Jehovah.

Samuel also identifies the one who spoke to Gideon as "the angel of the Jehovah" (Judges 6:12 ASV). Manoah and his wife saw the Angel of Jehovah and feared they would die, because they had seen God (Judges 13:21–22). So also this angel is identified as Jehovah in Zechariah's vision (compare 3:1 with 3:2; *Lord* in NASB and NKJV)

We conclude that the Angel of Jehovah was a theophany, an appearance of God in visible and bodily form before the incarnation. He appeared to manifest God's person and purpose to His people.

Though this Angel of Jehovah (the Lord) is identified as Jehovah, he also is distinct from Jehovah. Some might call that an impasse, a logical barrier for the human mind. Is this a contradiction in terms? No; the difficulty has a resolution, as we will see shortly. Yet we must acknowledge that the angel is distinct from Jehovah in two ways.

First, the angel intercedes to Jehovah (the Lord). Zechariah 1:8–10 presents a vision of a man among the myrtle trees. He seems to be the leader of a patrol of angelic beings. Verse 11 equates him with the angel of Lord (*Yaweh*). But now, in verse 12, the Angel of Jehovah (Lord) appeals to one he addresses as "O Lord of hosts" to have compassion on Jerusalem and the cities of Judah. Here is Jehovah speaking to another Jehovah. These two persons are obviously distinct.

Second, the angel calls upon Jehovah. Zechariah 3 presents the vision of a courtroom scene. Joshua, the high priest, represents sinful Israel; whereas Satan stands at Joshua's right hand accusing him (3:1). Then the Lord (*Yaweh*) "said to Satan, 'The Lord rebuke you, Satan! Indeed, the Lord who has chosen Jerusalem rebuke you!'" The only one who could be called Lord of the three who were present in the courtroom is the Angel of Jehovah. Yet he appeals to Jehovah as the judge to rebuke Satan. Again we see the Angel of Jehovah as distinct from Jehovah. This might present an unsolvable mystery to some.

We can solve the mystery if we allow that Jehovah God exists as a composite unity, as a triune God. *His identity is with Christ.*

Christ's essential nature is that of genuine and complete deity. This is the clear presentation of the New Testament (John 1:1–2; Colossians 2:9; 3:1). We see in Matthew 28:18–19 that all persons of the Trinity—Father, Son, and Holy Spirit—have the same name or authority. Even the Old Testament implicitly presents this concept. In Deuteronomy, the famous *shema Israel* calls upon God's people to recognize that He is one God. Here Moses uses the word *echod,* the same word used to describe the large bunch of grapes brought back by the spies from their investigation of the Promised Land (Numbers 13:23). This indicates a composite unity. The word for "one" in the *shema* is also used in Genesis 2:24 of God designing Adam and Eve to become "one flesh." They do not lose personal identity in this composite relationship.

Isaiah quotes God as saying, "I am He, I am the first, I am also the last" (48:12). This same one says, "And now the Lord God *(Yaweh)* has sent Me, and His Spirit" (48:16). He further describes Himself as "the Lord, your Redeemer, the Holy One of Israel" (48:17). There is good evidence that God exists as a tri-unity—three persons in one godhead.

If we allow this, then we can better understand and solve the mystery of the Angel of Jehovah being identified as Jehovah and yet being distinct from Jehovah. Furthermore, we can then recognize the Angel of Jehovah's true identity: *He is the second person of the Trinity, the Son, the Lord Jesus Christ,* appearing before He became a member of the human race.

Remember, in the triune God's administration, the Son is subordinate to the Father, and the Holy Spirit is subordinate to both the Father and the Son. The Lord Jesus said both "I and the Father are one" (John 10:30) and, "The Father is greater than I" (John 14:28). The Lord Jesus was sent by the Father to do His will (John 6:38). The Lord Jesus voluntarily took on responsibilities to accomplish redemption.

With this in mind, there are four reasons to identify the Angel of Jehovah as Christ in preincarnate appearances:

1. The Son is the visible God of the New Testament (John 1:14, 18; 14:9); so the Son was the visible representative of God in the Old Testament.
2. The appearances of this angel ceased after the Son's incarnation. (Matthew 1:20 should be taken as an angel of the Lord.)
3. They both were sent by God and had similar ministries, such as revealing, guiding, and judging. The Father was never sent.
4. This angel could not be the Father or the Holy Spirit. Neither one ever takes bodily form (John 1:18; 3:8).

The Angel of Jehovah, often translated as "the Angel of the Lord," may be understood as being the preincarnate Son. His appearances before His human birth in Bethlehem provide evidence that Christ's activities have been from old, from everlasting (Micah 5:2). This angel is no ordinary angel!

Dear Lord Jesus, thank You for Your concern for Your people in the Old Testament days. You are truly Jehovah God along with the Father, and I worship You. Thank You for taking genuine human form and living among us. You revealed the Father and You rescued Your people, then and now. Please remind me of Your love and intervention in my life as I commit my heart and paths to You. Amen.

The Angel of Jehovah:
His Ministries

Then the angel of the Lord answered and said, "O Lord of hosts, how long will You have no compassion for Jerusalem and the cities of Judah . . . ?" (Zechariah 1:12)

The ministries of the Angel of Jehovah [the Lord] were many and varied. As God's representative to His people in the Old Testament, this angel paralleled those of Christ in the New Testament. Here we will just list them briefly. (A further study may be found in *Angels, Elect and Evil.*)

The Angel of Jehovah and Jesus each presented revelation, commissioned His people, delivered from servitude, protected those who trust God, interceded for His people, and acted as advocate for them. Each also confirmed covenants, comforted the brokenhearted, and acted as judge. These parallel ministries support the identity of the Angel of Jehovah as being the preincarnate Christ.

The Angel of Jehovah had several other likely ministries. These included calling to faith and commitment, giving provision and safekeeping, offering forgiveness and direction, representing God's presence, appearing in the glory cloud that led Israel, and acting as the leader of God's armies.

When we think of the Angel of Jehovah, we can thank God for His firm and unchanging care for His people. The angel ministered widely and effectively. God intervened at times of great need, such as delivering Israel from Egyptian bondage, leading Israel through its wilderness wanderings, acting as the Captain who led Joshua and Israel into the Promised Land, overthrowing Midian's oppression of Israel, and encouraging Joshua and Zerubbabel in restoring Israel after their Babylonian captivity.

Similarly, the Lord Jesus has promised never to leave us or forsake us. He will guide us through our earthly journey. He will provide for us and protect us from evil. He will grant us victory over all our enemies, and He will see us through to our inheritance—association with Him in His glory.

In His incarnation, the eternal Son of God experienced human form. As the eternal Son with permanent humanity, He is better than an occasional appearance of a very special messenger, such as the Angel of Jehovah. He represented us on the cross, a perfect human sacrifice that could atone for our sins, and He now represents us as our High Priest in heaven. One day He will appear again to reign on earth forever as our King, our Friend, our

Sufficiency, and our Hope forever. Hallelujah (praise Yaweh)! What a Savior!

Thank You, Lord Jesus, for Your many ministries for Your people Israel and for Your church. You call us to faith and commitment. You intercede with the Father for us and defend us from the accusations and intrusions of Satan. For this I praise You and trust You to care for me and for my concerns. Amen.

Chapter 6

NAMES
OF SATAN

We cannot consider the names of angels without looking at the names of Satan and demons. They are fallen angels and play a significant role in history and in the present world scene. They seek the ruin of mankind, but particularly those who belong to Christ. Their names give insight into their power and activity.

In the next four chapters, we will look at several names of Satan and his followers who are in rebellion against God. We will learn of their goals and deceptions, as well as the resources available to oppose them. In this chapter we will consider these names for Satan:

- The Ruler of This World
- The God of This World
- The Ruler of Demons

Satan's Reality

You are of your father the devil, and you want to do the desires of your father. He was a murderer from the beginning, and does not stand in the truth because there is no truth in him. (John 8:44)

When it comes to the subject of Satan and demons, there are two extremes to avoid: (1) Satan is all myth, and (2) Satan is all mighty. The Bible presents Satan as a real spirit being, a fallen creature who once was beautiful but now is corrupt and evil in character and conduct; yet he is subject to God's authority. No matter how powerful he is, Satan is still God's creature and subject to God's authority. Satan is not a symbol of evil or a composite of human wickedness. He is an angelic *person* of wide and powerful influence.

Satan continues to play a major role in the moral struggle of God's world. He hates God and mankind made in God's image. He especially hates those who have trusted Christ. We should know of him, respect him, and resist him in the faith and in the power of the Lord Jesus.

Many recognize the reality of angels, but how many think of Satan and demons as personal realities affecting individual and national experiences and futures? Yet evidence of his involvement in personal and world affairs is found in the Old Testament, the New Testament, and the words of Jesus Christ Himself.

Old Testament evidence. The Old Testament assumes the reality of Satan, much as it does the reality of God. There is no formal proof set forth for either one, but their reality is obvious. The whole story of the Bible depends upon the reality of God and Satan for its development.

In Genesis 1 and 2, we see God creating the world and the human race. Immediately there follows the attack by a morally perverted creature that caused the first sin and the fall of the entire race. The rest of the Bible depicts a battle between good and evil, righteousness and sin, God and Satan. The whole redemptive plan of God developed in the Old Testament is centered in the God-man, the coming Messiah, who overcomes Satan and frees those in the race of mankind who trust in Him.

It seems strange that even some evangelical Christians do not recognize Satan as speaking through the serpent in the garden. They suppose that animals could talk before the fall. There is not one shred of evidence for this concept. Only those made in God's image have the gift of language, the most complicated function of the human race. Note that the argument of the serpent (Genesis 3:1–5) is a moral attack upon the character and command of God. Furthermore, Jesus refers to Satan as a murderer and liar from the beginning (John 8:44). Revelation 12:9 speaks of "the great dragon . . . the serpent of old who is called the devil and Satan." What well-known ancient serpent is in view if not the one in the garden?

The whole story of the suffering and relief of Job, one of the earliest stories written, depends on the prologue in chapters 1 and 2 where God challenges Satan. Furthermore, demonic realities are pictured as promoting idolatrous worship, even infant sacrifice, in Psalms 106:36–37 and 109:6. The unusual position and powers of the king of Babylon in Isaiah 14:1–17 and the king of Tyre in Ezekiel 28:1–19 are difficult to explain without the backing of a personal Satan. Zechariah 3 presents a supernatural adversary accusing Joshua and Israel who is opposed by the Angel of Jehovah, the preincarnate Son of God. (See Chapter 5.)

In the Old Testament, Satan is depicted as a real creature who is under God's control and judgment. Although a great fallen angel, He is no threat to God and no match for God's power.

New Testament evidence. Satan's existence is recognized by every writer of the New Testament, though not by every book. Nineteen of the twenty-seven books mention Satan by one of his names. Four more imply his reality by mentioning demons.

Evidence from Christ. The Lord Jesus is responsible for twenty-five of the twenty-nine references to Satan in the Gospels. Christ deals with Satan as a real person. In the temptation, Jesus carries on a moral argument with Satan, both of them using Scripture (Luke 4:1–13). It was Christ who reported this story to the apostles so they could write of it. The resistance and victory of Christ demonstrates that He is morally fit to be the Messiah and Savior.

Great Father God, I recognize Your reality and Your presence in my life. I trust no one except the Lord Jesus for my eternal salvation and for my present well-being. Thank You that though the enemy is real and strong, You are infinitely great and kind and intervening. You will protect and guide me in Your way. Amen.

Satan's Nature

And the great dragon was thrown down, the serpent of old who is called the devil and Satan, who deceives the whole world; he was thrown down to earth and his angels were thrown down with him. (Revelation 12:9)

What kind of being is Satan? According to the Bible, he has personhood; he was a magnificent person created by God who rebelled. He also is a creature, a spiritual being with great power.

Let's consider *his personhood.* Satan has the traits of personhood. He *thinks* in a moral sphere. His great intellect is found in his scheming to deceive personal minds (2 Corinthians 11:3) and in his speaking to other persons (Luke 4:1–12). He also *feels;* his emotions desire to elevate himself above God (Isaiah 14:12–17) and defeat Christ (Luke 4:1-12). In fury, he seeks to destroy God's people, the Jewish nation, and those who protect them (Revelation 12:12, 17). Satan also *chooses;* his will appealed to Christ's will to obey him (Luke 4:3, 9). He willfully still rebels against God (Revelation 20:7–9).

Significantly, the Scriptures use *personal* pronouns to describe Satan. "You were the anointed cherub who covers, and I placed you there. . . . And you sinned" (Ezekiel 28:14, 16). "Satan disguises himself as an angel of light," the apostle Paul writes (2 Corinthians 11:14). James commands, "Submit therefore to God. Resist the devil and he will flee from you" (James 4:7). He is a person as are the other persons in context.

God holds Satan as *morally responsible,* another sign this angel has personhood. God does not judge impersonal animals or forces, just persons created in His image. The Cross judged Satan, and he will end up in the Lake of Fire (John 16:11; Matthew 25:41).

Next, consider his *constitution*. Satan is a *creature*. He cannot be compared with God. However, God created him as a magnificent person. "You were blameless in your ways from the day you were created until unrighteousness was found in you" (Ezekiel 28:15). He owes his very existence to the Christ that he opposes (Colossians 1:16). He is infinitely less than God and very limited.

He also is a *spirit being* of the cherubim class (Ezekiel 28:14, 16). He doesn't have a body and should not be pictured as some terrifying or clownish man with a red suit and pitchfork. He is an awesome person of high, if not highest, class.

He seems *first in rank among all angels*. He was "the *anointed* cherub," the head of God's honor guard. His special position is expressed by *anointed*, which was used of kings. His perfection made his sin all the more horrible (Ezekiel 28:12).

Satan is real. As we will see, his activity is deceptive and destructive. He leads humans into the bondage of sin and slavery to his will. He still retains some dignity but is thoroughly perverted and no longer beautiful. We need to be aware of his schemes to protect ourselves from his ruinous activity. We should respect his person and power, but we need not shrink from him in fear. Those in Christ have a position of authority far above him and demons (Ephesians 1:19–2:6). Though retaining great power, Satan is no match for God and His Messiah.

*Lord Jesus, Creator of all, including all spirit be-
ings, I thank You that You are in charge of all things,
even evil beings. I know they are not a threat to You and
that You protect us from the Evil One. He owes his very
existence to You, and You will show Your power in controlling him and finally confining him to everlasting
fire. Show us Your power today in keeping us from
temptation that would lead us into defeat by Satan's de-
vices. Keep us alert and depending on You. Amen.*

The Ruler of This World

*Now judgment is upon this world; now the ruler
of this world will be cast out.* (John 12:31)

Of course, we understand that God did not create
evil angels. He is light and there is no darkness in
Him at all (1 John 1:5). He does no evil, nor can He.
The angel we are considering is the one God created
and positioned as "the anointed cherub who covers
[guards]" (Ezekiel 28:14). We are well aware of the
name *cherub,* the singular of *cherubim* (see chapter
4). It refers to Satan's original position assigned by
God as the highest ranking guardian of God's glory.
He sought to replace God as the ruler of all. How he
has fallen! What a waste of his power and potential!
Any creature, angel or human, who rebels against
God wastes his life and possibilities capable under
the Creator's good provision and direction (Matthew
16:26).

Jesus called this creature "the ruler of this
world." Satan rules an ordered system (Greek, *cosmos*) that includes men and angels aligned against
God (Matthew 12:14; John 8:44; Romans 8:7–8).
This *cosmos* is Satan's kingdom that opposes God's

kingdom program. He wanted to be like "the Most High" (Isaiah 14:14), not in character but in control. Now he energizes human rebels and promotes false religions (Ephesians 2:1–2).

He seeks to defeat the children of God. When we love what the world system offers—pleasure, possessions, and prestige—we do not love the Father; we fall into Satan's trap (1 John 2:15–17). Let us take a stand against deceptive, degrading, and destructive loves. How impoverished are the riches of the world!

Satan is also named "the prince of the power of the air," (Ephesians 2:2). This name could mean "the authoritative prince of the air," or "the prince of the empire of this atmosphere." It pictures Satan as the ruler of a kingdom that operates where we live and breathe. In Ephesians 2:2, it is connected with the *cosmos*. This kingdom promotes a philosophy and lifestyle of creature-centered power and comfort.

Even believers can be drawn to worldly attitudes and behaviors. Satan constantly pours forth energy into his subjects (Ephesians 2:2), activating them, just as God would pour His energy into those who follow Christ (Philippians 2:13).

Dear Father God, keep me from any form of following the ruler of this world. I know that to love the world is to reject Your love for me. Deliver me from buying into the philosophy of the world system aligned against my loving Father. I sacrifice my comforts and my goals to Your good and perfect plan. In Jesus' name, amen.

The God of This World

And even if our gospel is veiled, it is veiled to those who are perishing, in whose case the god of this world has blinded the minds of the unbelieving, so that they might not see the light of the gospel of the glory of Christ, who is the image of God. (2 Corinthians 4:3–4)

Though he is not God, Satan is described as "the god of this *world*" (2 Corinthians 4:4). He intends to destroy humans, to keep them on the road to judgment, by blinding their minds. The term here translated *world* is the Greek word *aion*, which could be understood as *age-spirit*, or *spirit of the age*. It includes what the philosophy of a culture holds important while living separated from God. This includes what self-centered humans, driven by demons, hold to be the essence and goal of life.

Through the centuries, the particular expression of this creature-centered philosophy has varied; empiricism, rationalism, existentialism, and nihilism have been among the philosophies. Today postmodern thought seems to reign. Behind them all has been the same heart—one independent of the true and living God. Each "age-spirit" has a counterfeit and destructive lifestyle that forsakes the true life in Christ for the false life colored by human and satanic sin. Thought systems at times have even been religious, yet the "age-spirit" is always antichrist and under the judgment of God. We need to examine our values and priorities lest we fall into the trap of the enemies of God.

Standing behind the human scene is the *god of this age.* He orchestrates his philosophy in human minds. His view finds expression in education, history, philosophy, medicine, art, theater, and religion too. All are infected with a false worldview and deviate from God's truth.

Satan "has blinded the minds of the unbelieving," wrote the apostle Paul, in order to keep them from recognizing the light and embracing the truth of the gospel of Christ (2 Corinthians 4:4). No wonder! Satan hates God and Christ. Since he can't get at them, he seeks to harm humans made in God's image. Satan wants to keep humans trapped in sin's clutches that they may end up with him in his horrible destiny—eternal torment and separation from God.

We are vulnerable to Satan's schemes and power. He specializes in mind control. He spreads his propaganda in all forms of thought and pursuits to keep us from Christ and His truth.

The truth, the way, and the light of life are found only in the Person and work of the Lord Jesus. He is "the light of the world" (John 8:12). He alone can deliver from sin's penalty and grant eternal life (John 14:6; 5:24).

We need to trust the Lord Jesus to release us from sin and Satan. When we do, God transfers us from the kingdom of darkness into the kingdom of God's dear Son (Colossians 1:13). At that point, there is assurance: We will never be separated from God and His love (Romans 8:35–39). But even believers can be led astray from the simplicity of devotion to Christ. The apostle Paul was concerned lest Satan would beguile Corinthian believers through the mind-control schemes of false teachers (2 Corinthians 11:3–4, 13–15).

Trusting the Lord Jesus marks the beginning of

life. Then each believer needs to commit his or her life to Christ's leading and direction. We need transformation by the *renewing of our minds* in God's Word and in every one of our relationships (Romans 12:1–2). Only then will we be able to stand against the blinding and distracting force of the enemy's mind-control efforts.

Gracious Father, keep me from being blinded by Satan's destructive philosophy. I don't want to be trapped in the values established in this evil world system. Sensitize my mind and heart to embrace truth and avoid falsehood. I don't want to squander the life bought and graciously granted to me in Christ. I choose Your truth and Your values to govern my life. Looking forward to Christ's total triumph, I want to triumph by walking with Him now. In Jesus' name, amen.

The Ruler of Demons

Then a demon-possessed man who was blind and mute was brought to Jesus, and He healed him, so that the mute man spoke and saw. All the crowds were amazed, and were saying, "This man cannot be the Son of David, can he?" But when the Pharisees heard this, they said, "This man casts out demons only by Beelzebul the ruler of demons." (Matthew 12:22–24)

The world system that plays out the world's philosophy also includes demons under one named "the ruler of demons." The Pharisees accused Jesus of being in league with "Beelzebul, the ruler of the demons" (Luke 11:15; Matthew 12:24). Since His enemies could not deny His miracles, they sought to discredit Him and to void His claims by attributing His power over demons to their ruler, Satan.

Christ refuted the charge with logic and power. He claimed, instead, that He cast out demons by the Holy Spirit as evidence of His true Messiahship (Matthew 12:25–29).

Realizing himself not sufficient to overthrow God, Satan swept one-third of the angelic host away from God (Revelation 12:3–4). Now he rules over his angels, or demons, with absolute control. They fear and serve him with desperate hope of winning the battle. But God will cause the Lord Jesus to triumph (Matthew 25:41; Revelation 20:1–3, 10).

Beelzebul was the name of one of the gods of the Philistines and was used by the Hebrews as a title of Satan. Both the Pharisees and Jesus understood it that way. This was the same name as *Baal-zebub,* the god of Ekron, a Philistine city (2 Kings 1:3, 6, 16). Some think that *Baalzebub* ("lord of the flies," or "god of the dunghill") could be an intentional Hebrew insult of the Canaanite *Baalzebul* ("lord of the high place," or "exalted Baal"). To use this name of Satan as the source of Christ's miraculous power was a great insult to the pure and holy Son of God. Indeed, Jesus said it was blasphemy (Matthew 12:24, 31–32).

The Lord Jesus warned against blasphemy of the Holy Spirit. The Pharisees were attributing the work of the Holy Spirit to Satan. The unpardonable sin was to deny the deity of Jesus and equate the Holy Spirit with Satan, rejecting Christ totally. This sin cannot be committed today, because Christ is not personally here working miracles by the Holy Spirit. Even in Christ's day, He held out the possibility of a change of mind to His opponents (Matthew 12:36–37).

Though these names of Satan reflect his position and speak of Satan's great power and authority, the Lord Jesus easily binds this strong one; He is the Son of God who did cast out demons by the Spirit of God (Matthew 12:28–29). Today the risen Jesus has authority over all opposition (Matthew 28:18).

Though Satan cannot continue without the permission of God, he still uses his power to seek to undo the work of God and to ruin the lives of men and women. Let us keep alert and resist his attempts to ruin us. We can stand against the power of the ruler of demons as those who have been raised and seated with Christ in heavenly places, far above all of Satan's evil armies (Ephesians 1:19–2:6a).

Powerful Savior, I thank You that You stand in complete authority and control over all the forces of evil. Your Word says that nothing can separate me from Your love. Keep me by Your grace and power from the inroads of evil spirits. I thank You that I am seated with You in the heavenly places far above my enemies. I want to assume that position every day. Alert me to the first approach of evil so that I may stand in Your power and Your truth against every attempt to lead me astray. I praise You for Your saving and keeping power. Amen.

Chapter 7

NAMES THAT REVEAL
SATAN'S CHARACTER

Many parents consult books on the meaning of children's names before naming their children; they learn, for example, that Andrew means *brave* and Emily means *industrious*. Names often can reveal intended or actual character of the person. Thus Abram (Genesis 11:27) means "exalted father," and God renamed him Abraham (Genesis 17:5) to reflect the type of exaltation he would have. Abraham means "father of a great number."

Similarly, many of the names of Satan, including the name *Satan* itself, reveal his character. As we look at the following names, we will learn how Satan was once the shining one who fell deeply into sin and today remains what he became shortly after his fall: a crafty, deceiving serpent, a ruthless dragon and destroyer of souls, and an angel full of evil.

- Lucifer
- Satan
- The Devil
- The Serpent of Old
- The Great Dragon
- The Destroyer
- The Evil One

Lucifer

*How you are fallen from heaven, O Lucifer, son of
the morning! How you are cut down to the ground, you
who weakened the nations!* (Isaiah 14:12 NKJV)

The silent films of the early twentieth century often
were melodramas in which the fair lady was beset
by the schemes of the villain. He was an unscrupu-
lous, evil man who preyed upon the weak and unsuspecting. The hero always rescued the heroine
just in the nick of time. The audiences would move
from tenseness and horror to relief and applause
when the villain's schemes were undone. "Villain"
was a name that depicted the character of this
sneaky, ravenous one who threatened the life and
welfare of good people.

Satan has several names that depict his character. They are names we should know, because God
has revealed and recorded them in the Scriptures.
They warn us of this "villain" who schemes to attack us.

The name *Lucifer* is the Latin equivalent for the
Hebrew *hilel*, and it refers to this angel as "the shining one." *Lucifer* describes Satan in his original state
—before he fell in his rebellion against God—as
full of light and reflecting the beauty in which God
had created him. The New American Standard
Bible translates this as "star of the morning," and
the text further calls him "son of the dawn." Those
phrases may imply that he was first in time or first
in position in the dawn, the beginning, of creation.

How wonderfully the Shining One displayed
the magnificence of God's creativity. Ezekiel further
explained this beauty, as the Lord God addressed

him in 28:12–19 as behind the king of Tyre. Verses 12–13 are full of superlatives:

> You had the seal of perfection, full of wisdom and perfect in beauty. You were in Eden, the garden of God; every precious stone was your covering: the ruby, the topaz, and the diamond; the beryl, the onyx, and the jasper; the lapis lazuli, the turquoise, and the emerald; and the gold, the workmanship of your settings and sockets, was in you. On the day that you were created they were prepared.

He is further addressed as "the anointed cherub who covers" or guards (28:14). God speaks of Lucifer's created and provisional holiness in verse 15: he was "Blameless . . . until unrighteousness was found in you." The cause for Satan's sin is set before us in verse 17: "Your heart was lifted up because of your beauty; you corrupted your wisdom by reason of your splendor. I cast you to the ground; I put you before kings, that they may see you."

It was pride in his beauty and occupation with his donated dignity, and perhaps in his high station, that caused Lucifer, the shining one, to fall. And in falling, he turned from light into darkness and from holiness into corruption. What a waste! To think that with such wisdom, beauty, and power, the creature who was designed to reflect the light and truth of God would turn against his creator, provider, and friend! Surrounded by other holy angels and privileged to enjoy the presence and fellowship of the true and living God, the shining one became the darkened one. Now satanists are proud to call him Lucifer, duped by the false light into death and destruction. They hold to his lying promises that he will give them power and pleasure when he finally wins the battle against Christ. But Satan and demons know that they shall find their eternal judgment and torment in the Lake of Fire. And it is the Lord Jesus Christ who shall cast them there (Matthew 25:41).

And as it was with Satan, so it was with humans. Not trusting God for all they needed, and choosing against His command and His fellowship, Adam and Eve rebelled against God. Created in His image and given great provisions, privileges, and position, they were not satisfied. They believed the lie that God was holding out on them and that they could be like Him. Isn't that reflective of Satan's desire, "I will be like the Most High"?

Satan still sows the same propaganda today, no matter what the form. "You can master your own life," says the humanist. "You are sleeping gods. Wake to your innate potential," proclaims the New Age teacher. "I did it my way," sings the old crooner. And what could be beautiful and reflective of God's creative light becomes dark and twisted, stuck in the mire of self-sufficiency and self-satisfaction, hurting others—it becomes villainous.

Only the Savior, the Lord Jesus, can rescue us, taking our feet from miry clay and setting our feet upon the solid rock of His righteousness and grace. Those who will not receive Christ but oppose His righteousness and grace shall join the fallen Lucifer in the Lake of Fire (John 8:24; Matthew 25:41).

Father in heaven, You made all things beautiful—all angels, all the world, even humans. Thank You that

You made me in Your image, a beautiful person. But I am stained with sin and often act in rebellion. Often I, too, want to do things my way. Help me to humbly face my helplessness and hopelessness apart from You. I want to be occupied with You, my Creator, Sustainer, Redeemer, and Friend. I depend on You to enable me to love You and serve Christ faithfully. Amen.

Satan

Now there was a day when the sons of God came to present themselves before the Lord, and Satan also came among them. (Job 1:6)

Though we have previously mentioned this name of our enemy, we have not specifically treated its meaning. *Satan* comes transliterated from the Hebrew *satan*. It means "the opposer, the adversary." It is found first in the early story of Job (1:6; 2:1). God calls all "the sons of God" (Hebrew, *bene elohim*) before Him, and Satan is among them. He is identified as an angel, a strong one; but he is fallen. Here he is opposing God and Job.

This common name, *Satan,* is used fifty-two times in the Bible, typically as wanting to be the rival of God. In wanting to be like the Most High, he has set up a counterfeit and rival kingdom in the world system. As the leader of such an opposition, he hates God and God's people (Zechariah 3:1–2). Right from the beginning, he lured Adam and Eve away from God's fellowship and service. He is identified as working through the serpent and is labeled "the ancient serpent, called the Devil and Satan" (Revelation 12:9).

But just as in Zechariah's vision when the Angel of Jehovah defended His people, so the Lord Jesus today defends us, even when we have sinned; He protects us from the Adversary. The apostle John encourages us with these words: "My little children, I am writing these things to you that you may not sin. And if anyone sins, we have an Advocate with the Father, Jesus Christ the righteous; and He Himself is the propitiation for our sins; and not for ours only, but also for those of the whole world" (1 John 2:1–2).

As our God-appointed defense lawyer rises and defends us, He is not called "Jesus Christ the excuse maker." There are reasons but no excuses for our sins. And He is not called "Jesus Christ the eloquent," as if He could somehow with words change the picture. After all, God knows all things perfectly. Nor is He called "Jesus Christ the clever lawyer," as if He would put something over on the Judge of all. After all, Jesus is the way and the truth. He could not lie. But as He rises and defends His erring children, even before they confess their sins, He is called "Jesus Christ the righteous."

In perfect justice and in accord with truth, He points to the cross where He paid our penalty to God's full satisfaction. His blood speaks forgiveness and justification before God the Judge. And the Father God, who appointed Him and is the Judge, answers with a decisive "Amen!" How we need to thank the Father for such effective defense against our adversary, Satan.

Dear heavenly Father, I know You can fully handle Your adversary and mine. You call him to answer to You. You silence his claims against me when I sin. Thank You for appointing the ultimate defense lawyer,

Jesus Christ, Your Son. Since His sacrifice fully satisfies You, and I have been fully forgiven the condemning guilt of my sin, I boldly come to confess my daily sins and to receive full cleansing to enjoy Your fellowship and enablement. I praise Your holy name. In Jesus' name, amen.

The Devil

Finally, be strong in the Lord and in the strength of His might. Put on the full armor of God, so that you will be able to stand firm against the schemes of the devil. For our struggle is not against flesh and blood.
(Ephesians 6:10–12a)

When I once was preaching about Satan in a Protestant church of reformational descent, a man came to me after the evening service protesting: "If I had been in Salem, you would have hanged me. I can't believe that anyone in the twentieth century would think that there are a personal devil and demons!" I answered him that his argument was not with me, but with the Scriptures and with the Lord Jesus for which his church stood.

If we hold to a humanistic and materialistic worldview, then the reality of the devil and demons makes little sense. But the Bible uses the common name *the devil* thirty-five times. The Greek *diabolos* means "slanderer," or "one who trips up." The devil maliciously utters false reports that slander and are designed to injure the life and reputation of others. He seeks to defame God and believers. The apostle Peter warns us, "Be of sober spirit, be on the alert. Your adversary, the devil, prowls about like a roaring lion, seeking someone to devour" (1 Peter 5:8). The connection in context speaks of humbling ourselves before God and "casting all your anxiety upon Him, because He cares for you" (5:6–7).

The devil seeks to trip us up with fears and anxieties. He attacks us in our weakness, since we are creatures with limitations and sinners with inadequate and false concepts of God. He wants to make us think that God is harsh or, at least, not concerned about our real needs. Then he can move us to act contrary to God's will and concern for us. Peter knew of the devil's work along this line. Jesus warned him about the devil's desire to work Peter over, but Christ prayed for him that his faith should not fail (Luke 22:31–32). How good to know that Jesus cares and is praying for us even now.

Dear Father in heaven, I thank You that You constantly care for me and my concerns. I cast all my cares upon You and will not leave them as toeholds for the devil to climb upon to control my mind and emotions. Help me to think magnificently about You and Your concerns for me. Keep me from moving contrary to Your will, and keep me trusting You. And don't let me join the devil's work in accusing or slandering others. In Jesus' name, amen.

The Serpent of Old

And the great dragon was thrown down, the serpent of old who is called the devil and Satan, who deceives the whole world. (Revelation 12:9)

Not too long ago, California citizens feared "the night stalker" who murdered young women for seemingly the fun and thrill of it. We stand aghast at such treachery and wanton taking of human life. But if we recall the biblical records, we should not be completely baffled by the evil that infects the human race. Satan murdered the whole race with his lies to Eve and to Adam. Then their child Cain murdered his brother, Abel. We read in 1 John 3:12 that Cain "was of the evil one, and slew his brother. . . . Because his deeds were evil. . . ."

The name *serpent of old*, recalls Satan's first appearance in the biblical record. He stalked Eve in the garden and caused the human race to fall in Adam's sin (Genesis 3). What could the term *of old* or *ancient* mean except the only well-known reference to an opponent of God called a serpent. Snakes do not talk. There is no evidence for such a wild conjecture. Among earthly creatures, only humans learn and use complicated language and use it in a moral context. Of course, so can Satan. He used human language in communicating with Christ in His temptations. There was no need for John to clarify his use of "serpent" as referring to Satan.

Elsewhere, Paul wrote of his concern regarding teaching contrary to the biblical concept of Christ and His salvation: "But I am afraid, lest as the serpent deceived Eve by his craftiness, your minds should be led astray from the simplicity and purity of devotion to Christ" (2 Corinthians 11:3). Later in the same context, he refers to false apostles who are the servants of Satan (11:13–15).

The identification of the serpent with Satan is quite clear. The characteristic of Satan that stands out in this name is *crafty deception*.

As noted before, the Lord Jesus referred to Satan as a murderer and liar from the beginning (John 8:44; see also chapter 8). He murdered the race with a lie. Cain followed with his own expression of hatred. Some modern critics hold that we should not understand more than what could have been understood by the Hebrews of the day of the Scripture's writing. Yet the Fall of mankind is quite clearly due to evil, supernatural intervention. And does not God's progressive revelation clarify His previous revelation? The New Testament makes it obvious to the unbiased reader that *the ancient serpent* is the deceiver, Satan, with death-dealing venom under his tongue.

Let us guard ourselves against deception that so easily overcomes many. Paul was concerned for the Corinthians who had trusted Christ. Deceiving teachers, enabled by demons, sought to complicate the gospel with a works-righteousness salvation. This would deny the finished work of the Lamb of God and bring disgrace upon His sacrifice on the cross (Galatians 2:21). Let us guard our minds by a proper view of Christ as the God-man who purchased our full pardon and perfected our standing forever before a righteous God (Hebrews 10:12, 14).

Lord God, we cannot understand why Adam and Eve, blessed with all that they needed, would turn against You. You gave them a choice, and they chose against You when our enemy enticed them. We, too, left to our own resources and enticed by the old serpent, would also defect from our loving Father. May we daily confess our weakness and urgently implore You to keep us in Your way and to keep us from the evil one, just as Jesus taught us to pray. We trust You and Your grace for all we need. Amen.

The Great Dragon

And another sign appeared in heaven: and behold, a great red dragon. . . . And his tail swept away a third of the stars of heaven, and threw them to the earth.
(Revelation 12:3–4)

With the use of the name *the great dragon* (Revelation 12:9), the true character of the serpent comes to light. He is a terrifying, destructive beast whose rage against God and His people seeks to devastate them. Besides "the great dragon," he is also called "great red dragon" and "dragon" (Revelation 12:3–4, 9). In the context of the Great Tribulation, he leads an army of his angels in a war of destruction against the Messiah and His people, Israel (verses 4, 9, 17). Verse 9 connects several names that identifies him with Satan. Verse 7 paints an awe-inspiring spiritual conflict, the likes of which has never yet been seen: "And there was war in heaven, Michael and his angels waging war with the dragon. The dragon and his angels waged war."

The outcome of this battle is never in doubt, however; for God supports his angels, and they must win. Satan and his angels "were not strong enough, and there was no longer a place found for them in heaven. And the great dragon was thrown down . . . and his angels were thrown down with him" (12:8–9).

No matter how ferocious or strong, the great red dragon is no match for God's army of angels led by Michael, the archangel; for God gives power and assures the victory over the evil one. We may have great confidence not only in the outcome of this future battle but also in the present conflict during our time. If we submit to God and resist the devil, he will flee from us (James 4:7). The battle may not be finished overnight, so the submission and the resistance must continue. But in the end, we must win the battle. If we stand in the authority and strength of Christ, and if we put on the full armor of God, then we will not fail (Ephesians 6:10–18). We shall overcome!

Great sovereign God and Father of our Lord Jesus Christ, we praise You for Your power and intervention in the affairs of the world and in our personal lives. If it were not so, Your plan would have failed; and we should have perished long ago. Thank You for Your personal concern and Your sustaining grace. Thank You also for Your great army of angels and their involvement in world affairs and in our lives. Keep us trusting You. Amen.

The Destroyer

They have as king over them, the angel of the abyss; his name in Hebrew is Abaddon, and in the Greek he has the name Apollyon. (Revelation 9:11)

In Revelation 9:1–11, the apostle John describes grotesque demons who look like locusts and have the stinging power of scorpions. The demons also are compared to horses prepared for battle, and they have faces like men and wear golden crowns on their heads. They have teeth like lions, breastplates of iron, and their wings are like the noise of chariot horses running into battle. What a horrific scene of the Great Tribulation!

At the command of the fifth angel, who sounded his trumpet judgment from God, John saw "a star fallen from heaven." He was given permission to open the shaft of the abyss, and out came these destructive creatures. They are demons under their leader whose names *Abaddon* and *Apollyon* both mean "destroyer." This fallen angel, this king of the demons, is none other than Satan.

Satan is a destroyer of life. He sought to destroy God's reputation and rule. He seeks to destroy mankind and to kill those that belong to God, both of the Jews (Revelation 12:1–6) and of the church (2:8–11). Anti-Semitism and anti-Christian ideologies and practices are becoming the style of this age, whether in government, or media, or in general. Satan is goading on many rulers of this world today to persecute Christians and to bring many to martyrdom. Church historians report that there have been more martyrs for Christ in this century than in all the centuries combined from the start of the church.

Let us beware of the enemies, both demonic and human, who would destroy the church. Let us pray for those in leadership of the nations that we might live a godly and tranquil life. This will aid in more men coming to know Christ (1 Timothy 2:1–4). We can ask the Lord to remove from power those who oppose His truth and His people. "The weapons of our warfare are not of the flesh, but divinely powerful for the destruction of fortresses" (2 Corinthians 10:4). Prayer is one of the most powerful weapons we possess in our battle with Satan (Ephesians 6:13–18). Let us take the warfare seriously and battle our destructive foe with the resources of our risen and victorious Lord (Ephesians 6:10–12).

Lord Jesus, how hideous and destructive is the enemy! I'm so glad that in Your sovereignty You limit the powers of evil. You are the way, the truth, and the life. Guard Your people from the destroyer who would ravage our lives. Deliver us from ruination, but enable us to stand in the face of any pressure or persecution allowed to come our way. Keep me true to You, even if it means my reputation or my life. Defeat the work of Satan and his demons against the advance of the gospel and the building of Your church. I trust in Your grace and power. Amen.

The Evil One

I do not ask You to take them out of the world, but to keep them from the evil one. (John 17:15)

I can still see my dear mother baking bread and rolls. After mixing all the ingredients and before baking, she would allow the dough to rise. Then she would knead it, pound it down, and let it rise again until it was thoroughly affected by the yeast. You see, the yeast was a corrupting agent that decayed and produced gas to infiltrate all the dough. In this case, the outcome was good and delicious. However, yeast in the Bible speaks of the corruption of evil.

Jesus warned his disciples of evil legalistic teaching: "But beware of the leaven of the Pharisees and Sadducees" (Matthew 16:11). Paul warns us of the insidious spread of evil if allowed to continue in the church: "Your boasting is not good. Do you not know that a little leaven leavens the whole lump of dough?" (Galatians 5:9).

Jesus Himself gave this name, *the Evil One,* to Satan in His prayer just before He was betrayed and crucified. This Greek term, *ho poneros*, characterizes Satan as intrinsically wicked. He is not content to be himself corrupt, but he seeks to corrupt all around him. The whole world (Greek, *cosmos*) lies in the control and corruption of the evil one (1 John 5:19). The apostle John was confident that "no one who is born of God sins (Greek present tense, "practices sinning"); but He who was born of God keeps him and the evil one does not touch him" (5:18). The believer, as a rule, does not keep on sinning as a lifestyle. The Lord Jesus guards the believer so that Satan cannot grasp (Greek, *hapto*) him or drag him away from the Lord Jesus. What a good word for the security of the genuine believer in Christ. Security is Christ's job.

Guarding ourselves from sin and from idols is our job. We are to hate sin and to keep our lives from distraction and degradation associated with false gods (1 John 5:21). Our faith in Christ leads us to overcome the *cosmos* opposed to God. We do this by keeping God's commandments, which are not burdensome (5:3–4). Part of guarding ourselves from Satan is our daily prayer set forth by Christ in His pattern prayer of Matthew 6:9–13. We are to ask our heavenly Father for our daily bread, daily forgiveness, and for daily protection from the Evil One.

Keep me alert, Lord Jesus, to what You have labeled "evil." I don't want to be caught unaware by the schemes of the enemy. Guard my heart from the Evil One. Purify my lifestyle, and keep me from false gods and false pursuits. I want to live a genuine and attractive witness for the true and living God. Amen.

Chapter 8

NAMES THAT REVEAL SATAN'S ACTIVITIES

The various activities and strategies of Satan are apparent when we study other names given him in the Holy Scriptures. We have already learned that he is a cunning serpent and a cruel destroyer. Now we will be forewarned of his numerous strategies to mislead humans, such as temptation, accusation, lying, and deception. In this chapter we will see Satan as:

- The Tempter
- The Accuser
- The Liar and Deceiver
- The Spirit Working in the Disobedient

The Tempter

Then Jesus was led up by the Spirit into the wilderness to be tempted by the devil. . . . And the tempter came and said to Him, "If You are the Son of God, command that these stones become bread." (Matthew 4:1, 3)

In the barren Judean wilderness early in Jesus' ministry, Satan tempted the Son of God. They were alone; the tempter was isolating the Savior so that no one would be there to encourage Jesus. There were no disciples, no friends, no "reporters for the local paper"; just wild beasts. This story broke in the backside of the barren mountains.

As no one observed the confrontation, how did we get the account of what occurred? Jesus probably later recounted the story to His disciples. Through the Gospel writers Matthew, Mark, and Luke, the Lord Jesus reported the details of His encounter with Satan, whom He named "the tempter."

The Matthew account uses three names of the same person: "the devil" (Matthew 4:1), "Satan," (4:10), and "the tempter" (4:3). There is no doubt about whom Jesus is speaking. He is the same one who tempted Adam and Eve in the garden of Eden, the paradise of God. Yes, God allowed both temptations—that of the first Adam and that of the Last Adam, Jesus (1 Corinthians 15: 22, 45). As the two Adams, both were genuinely human, both were on earth because of special interventions of God, and both remain heads of a race of humans. Adam is the father and head of all our race in the physical sense. The Lord Jesus is the head of the race of all those who have trusted Him as personal Savior. There is quite a difference though. Adam was living in perfect circumstances, with a companion, and with all his needs being met by God. Christ was alone in difficult circumstances; He had been fasting forty days and then became very hungry and weak. He really needed the food that the tempter suggested He produce. Adam had all the garden's produce to satisfy him and his wife.

Satan thought he had Jesus in a hard place. However, Jesus was not merely a perfect human, as was Adam. He was the Word of God with a complete human nature. He was God-man; Satan had never met such a one before. Could he get Jesus to sin and ruin all the redemptive plan of God and tear the Son away from the Father? He didn't know for sure, but he surely tried with all his scheming powers.

The tempter knew Jesus' identity. The statement, "If you are the Son of God," does not reflect any doubt on Satan's certainty about who Jesus was. The Greek language here should be understood, "Since You are the Son of God, command that these stones become bread." The tempter asked him to do that which Christ could do—a miracle. But the Savior would not use His powers outside the will of God.

Instead, Jesus quoted the Scriptures; He lived by God's Word. Assuming the role of man under God's authority, He answered, "It is written, 'Man shall not live on bread alone, but on every word that proceeds out of the mouth of God'" (Matthew 4:4). In both ensuing temptations, Jesus obeyed the Word that He quoted. Thus He overcame the tempter.

What a great pattern for us when we are approached by temptation! We are to resist the tempter behind the temptations by obeying the Word of God. Do you know the Scriptures that apply to your weaknesses, your needs? Only by such a resource are we able to resist the devil. James 4:7 says, "Submit, therefore to God. Resist the devil and he will flee from you." And we need to remember 1 Corinthians 10:13: "No temptation has overtaken you but such as is common to man; and God is faithful, who will not allow you to be tempted beyond what you are able, but with the temptation will provide the way of escape also, that you may be able to endure it."

The tempter still seeks to lead followers of God into sinful disobedience. With the promises of God's Word, we can endure those temptations.

Lord Jesus, my gracious and faithful Savior, I thank You for keeping true to God and resisting the tempter. Help me to do the same in the strength that You provide. Lead me to the Word of God that will prepare me to meet the foe. I submit to You that I may then resist the devil. Keep me in Your way. Amen.

The Accuser

Then I heard a loud voice in heaven, saying, "Now the salvation, and the power, and the kingdom of our God and the authority of His Christ have come, for the accuser of our brethren has been thrown down, he who accuses them before our God day and night."
(Revelation 12:10)

Have you ever felt an oppressive, nagging reminder of some sin? It could be specific or just a vague, condemning feeling. Our consciences work according to a standard that may be true or false. Satan knows how we are constituted and how our minds work. He takes advantage of any weakness or ignorance. He kicks us when we are down. He is not active in heaven only, but also on earth. He not only accuses us before God, but he plays his war games with our minds. He promotes false guilt. That is why he is called "the accuser of [the] brethren" (Revelation 12:10).

Satan accused Job before God. That resulted in a spiritual battle that demonstrated the grace of God and the uprightness of Job. In that case, the accuser was defeated (Job 1:9–11; 2:4–5). Satan accused Joshua and Israel, but the Angel of the Lord defended them (Zechariah 3:1–2).

The full title and activity of the accuser is found in Revelation 12; the context is Satan's defeat by Christ and His holy angels during the Great Tribulation just before Christ's return. There Satan is called "the accuser of our brethren." It seems that humans in heaven are speaking these words, as "our brethren" indicates. There seems to be certain events upon earth that God allows believers in heaven to witness. At that time, the church-age saints will have been raptured or raised in glorified bodies. Then we will rejoice that the accuser, who has been active constantly until this defeat, is finally cast down; and his accusing has ended.

When the accuser protests that saints should be punished for their sin, the Father never considers the case valid. Of course believers sin. Of course God hates sin. But the Father has sent the Son to be the satisfaction for our sins (1 John 2:2). The Father has also appointed our defense lawyer, the Lord Jesus the righteous one, to defend us. He can do this with all moral freedom and rectitude, because He paid for our sins at the cross and now intercedes for us at the Judge's right hand (1 John 2:2). We can stand secure and with full assurance in the strong grace of God in Christ, so our consciences should not condemn us (Romans 8:33–39).

We need to stand against the tricks the accuser would play with our conscience. We can affirm our perfect standing before God. We can also confess our sins, not for the condemning guilt of sin, but for the family forgiveness from our Father. He forgives and cleanses so readily, but He keeps us even before we confess. Let's keep short accounts with God to enjoy His fellowship and His enabling in our lives.

Dear Father in heaven, I appreciate so much Your provision for my weakness and sinfulness. Please make me aware of the first approach of sin, so that I may avoid it. If I fail, please gently remind me of my sin, so that I may confess it and be restored to fellowship. I put on the full armor of God to stand against the devil's accusations. I especially appreciate the breastplate of Christ's righteousness, my perfect standing before You. Thank You, Lord Jesus, for Your heart and activity in defending me and keeping me secure and assured. Amen.

The Liar and Deceiver

You are of your father the devil, and you want to do the desires of your father. He was a murderer from the beginning, and does not stand in the truth because there is no truth in him. Whenever he speaks a lie, he speaks from his own nature; for he is a liar and the father of lies. (John 8:44)

Where did the practice of lying begin? It began right back in the Garden of Eden with the intrusion of Satan. Invading the perfect setting of holiness and satisfaction, the liar caught Eve's attention with a promise of more than she had. God was not sufficient. He was very restrictive. He was really afraid to let them know secret knowledge and secret power, lest they become like God. And they would not die (though God said they would).

This was the deceiver's tactic. Lies and deception marked each of his statements.

Satan knew the horrible results of seeking to be like the Most High (Isaiah 14:12–15). He was cast out of heaven, turning into a hideously evil person who opposes God's person, His program, and His people. So he attacked Adam and Eve through the lie and murdered all the race that descended from them. Now we all suffer through the liar's deception.

Currently Satan is the one "who deceives the whole world," a "deceiver" in his continuous activity. He will continue this strategy until he is bound during the messianic reign of Jesus. He will resume his deception upon a brief release at the end of the millennium (Revelation 20:3, 7–8).

The devil just never gives up, hoping, perhaps, that he can still somehow win. Either that, or he still seeks to take as many with him as possible, if he must go to "the lake of fire and brimstone," as John assures us (Revelation 20:10).

The liar/deceiver uses a wide range of scheming that has worked very well for him, from hiding his own existence to actively promoting false religions, philosophies, and morals. Sad to say, but many Christians are ignorant of the "schemes of the devil" (Ephesians 6:11). We need to receive the teachings and warnings of God's Word about this whole area that we might be able to avoid the pitfalls and ruination that the liar would bring upon us.

God of truth and light, guard me from the errors of my ways and from the deceptions of the enemy. Keep me walking in the light of Your Word, keeping sensitive to the Holy Spirit's working in my life. Let me listen to wise counsel and not think that I am sufficient in myself. Let me live and share the truth of the gospel and Your Word with others. In Jesus' name, amen.

The Spirit Working in the Disobedient

And you were dead in your trespasses and sins, in which you formerly walked according to the course of this world, according to the prince of the power of the air, of the spirit that is now working in the sons of disobedience. (Ephesians 2:1–2)

A soldier's disobedience in time of war is punishable by court-marshal. It may even result in execution. After all, lives are at stake, and rebellion against the commander endangers the whole campaign.

When King Saul intruded into the office of priest to offer sacrifice, he disobeyed the command of God. Saul's action was a self-serving move to keep his troops in a good mood and subservient to him. He also feared the Philistines assembled at Michmash to assault Israel. Yet in taking charge, even as king, he was rebelling against the orders of God. The prophet Samuel rebuked him for this sin: "You have acted foolishly; you have not kept the commandment of the Lord your God. . . . But now your kingdom shall not endure" (1 Samuel 13:13–14).

Just as we are, Saul was slow to learn the lesson. Subsequently, he did not obey the Lord's command to utterly destroy the Amalekites and all that they possessed (1 Samuel 15: 1–3, 8–9). Instead, he kept the best of the animals supposedly to sacrifice to the Lord (verse 21). Often we too forget that when we heed the spirit of disobedience, we engage in evil; we forget also that our obedience is much more important than any service to our God. As Samuel admonished the king, "Why then did you not obey the voice of the Lord, but rushed upon the spoil and did what was evil in the sight of the Lord?" (verse 19). He further admonished, "Behold, to obey is better than sacrifice, and to heed than the fat of rams. For rebellion is as the sin of divination, and insubordination is as iniquity and idolatry" (verses 22–23).

God hates disobedience. Yes, He loves His erring children, but He hates disobedience. It is the work of Satan. He constantly energizes those who are subject to his blinding and his deception. He enables those who are disobedient to the truth and to the gospel (Ephesians 2:2). The arch-rebel continually moves in human rebels to disobey God.

Now that we believers have been delivered from death and granted eternal life in Christ by the grace of God, how, then, should we continue in any form of disobedience to our gracious heavenly Father? Let us not displease Him with self-satisfaction and self-promotion. We actually reveal distrust in God's goodness and love when we act in rebellion.

My Father, my God, forgive me for taking things into my own hands and acting in ways contrary to Your commands. I repent and turn to You for forgiveness and cleansing. Heal my heart and direct my path in Your way. I have been translated from darkness to light and from death to life. Deliver me from the spirit that works in the disobedient. Let me live in obedience to You. In Jesus' name, amen.

Chapter 9

NAMES OF
EVIL ANGELS

Although the general public may believe in good angels, many are suspicious of the existence of evil angels, or demons. They tend to treat demons as they do Satan: a caricature and a myth that entertains occasionally in movies and on Halloween night. But like Satan, demons are real. They are mentioned more than one hundred times in the Old and New Testaments. Christ accepted the fact that Satan was the ruler of a host of demons (Matthew 24:41).

As we consider the reality and roles of demons, we need fear them no more than their leader, Satan, "because greater is he who is in you than he who is in the world" (1 John 4:4). We will be reminded once more of our great resources in Christ as we learn about the following names of evil angels:

- Demons
- Unclean Spirits
- Familiar Spirits
- The Devil's Angels
- Sons of God
- Spirits in Prison

Demons

And He healed many who were ill with various diseases, and cast out many demons; and He was not permitting the demons to speak, because they knew who He was. (Mark 1:34)

I was present on two occasions when two pastors, reacting to the subject someone introduced at the coffee table, said, "Don't talk to me about demons. It makes my flesh crawl!" If pastors fear, what shall the flock think? We need not fear; because the Lord Jesus, maker of all, is sovereign and cares for us. We fear because we do not know the truth nor the power of Christ.

That demons exist and that the Savior Jesus Christ has power over them is attested to throughout the Gospels. Christ put his messiahship and His casting out of demons on the same level of reality (Matthew 12:22–28). A large portion of Christ's ministry involved casting demons out of the demonized (Matthew 4:23–24). He gave his disciples authority to cast out demons (Matthew 10:1) and viewed His victories over them as those over Satan (Luke 10:17–18).

In His actions against the demons, Jesus was not accommodating the "ignorance of pre-scientific people," as some critics charge. He who is the way, the truth, and the life would not promote a false worldview. There really are demons who seek to extend Satan's influence and rule. He had rebuked a demon in a synagogue attender, saying, "Be quiet, and come out of him!" After throwing him into convulsions, the demon came out of the man. (Mark 1:25–26)

When the disciples could not relieve a boy who

had a demon that threw him into seizures, Jesus cast it out. When asked why they did not have success, Jesus did not explain the incident away as a psychosomatic trauma but explained, "Because of the littleness of your faith" (Matthew 17:20). He further said, "This kind cannot come out by anything but prayer" (Mark 9:29). He knew the real issue and had the right answer.

Demons are not the spirits of men of a pre-Adamic race, nor are they spirits of monstrous offsprings of angels and women. They are not spirits of ancestors come back to harass us. They are wicked angels who fell with Satan. There are similar expressions that support this: "the devil and his angels" (Matthew 25:41) and "Beelzebul the ruler of the demons" (Matthew 12:24), whom Jesus recognized as Satan (12:26). The term *ruler of the demons* indicates that Satan is first among the demons.

Since demons are fallen angels, they are spirit beings as well. They are called "evil spirits" (Luke 8:2) and have similar activities in opposing God and oppressing humans. They are creatures limited by God and will be judged by God. Believers in Christ have a position of authority far above all angels and demons (Ephesians 1:19–2:6). God has supplied all that we need for protection and direction in this fallen world.

Great Father God, I thank You for Your sovereign rule over all Your creation. No one thing is out of Your control. This comforts me and gives me confidence as I face the reality of evil in this world. I trust You, Lord Jesus, as the one who has all authority in heaven and

*earth, to keep me from the evil one and his demons. I
want You to be the sovereign Lord of my life and to
grant me grace and courage to face my foes, natural or
supernatural, in Your strength. In Jesus' name, amen.*

Unclean Spirits

*And they were all amazed, so that they debated
among themselves, saying "What is this? A new teaching with authority! He commands even the unclean
spirits, and they obey Him." (Mark 1:27)*

Just as angels are spirit beings, so are demons. The
apostle Paul contrasts them to humans with flesh
and blood (Ephesians 6:12). The fact that they are
spirit beings makes them persons, just as we noted
for angels. As such, they are merely creatures, limited in space, time, and powers. They are under the
sovereign jurisdiction of our Father God.

Demons are termed *unclean spirits* because they
are morally and spiritually unclean. Everything
about them is twisted and perverted. They use all
their intellect, emotions, and will against God and
His people. So we wrestle against "the rulers,
against the powers, against the world forces of this
darkness, against the spiritual forces of wickedness
in the heavenly places" (Ephesians 6:12). Some are
more wicked than others (Matthew 13:45). They
promote unclean lifestyles in perversion of religion
and of sexual conduct (Romans 1:21–27). Unrighteousness, wickedness, sensual living, murder, de-
ceit, rebellion, hatred, and violence often come
from the working of wicked spirits in the minds of
depraved men (Romans 1:28–32; 2 Peter 2:1–2,
13–14, 18–20).

Through men who forsake the truth of God's

Word, demons teach false and immoral doctrine
(1 Timothy 4:1–3). They empower those in the occult to perform miracle-like magic, such as did
Simon (Acts 8:9–10) and Elymas, whom Paul called
"you son of the devil" (Acts 13:8–11). Pharaoh's
magicians who opposed Moses with their magic
were also empowered by demons (2 Timothy 3:8).
We must be cautious, lest we think that all so-called
miracles are of God. The deceiver is at work, and
God does allow wicked, unclean spirits to confirm
humans in their evil ways. For instance, an evil
spirit troubled Saul because of his disobedience
(1 Samuel 16:14). God sent an evil spirit to mislead
the wicked king Ahab through the false prophets
(1 Kings 22:20–22).

We need not fear the enemies of our souls. God
is in charge and does all things well. All of Satan's
forces are infinitely below the exalted Lord Jesus
(Ephesians 1:19–21). Since we have trusted Christ,
we are raised and seated with Christ in heavenly
places far above all our spirit enemies (Ephesians
2:5–6). We have armor from God, and we can pray
against wicked, unclean spirits and their activity in
our lives. We can ask God to ruin their work in opposing us personally, His church, and the extension
of the gospel (Ephesians 6:18–20). We can ask the
Lord to ruin the activities and intents of the cults, the
occult groups, and those in witchcraft and satanism.

We are in a battle, and we have resources that
are effective in pulling down the enemy's strong-
hold (2 Corinthians 10:3–5).

*Lord Jesus, wake me up to the reality of wicked,
unclean spirits and their activities against me, Your*

people, and society in general. I choose not to fear them, but to trust You to keep me and mine from the evil ones, just as You prayed. I choose to trust in Your sovereign goodness and rest in Your authority as far above all wicked spirits. I will not participate in their practices of uncleanness. I commit my life to You in holiness. Teach me to pray pointedly against wickedness and uncleanness, and make me effective for You.

Familiar Spirits

And when they shall say unto you, Seek unto them that have familiar spirits, and unto wizards that peep, and that mutter: should not a people seek unto their God? for the living to the dead? To the law and to the testimony: if they speak not according to this word, it is because there is no light in them. (Isaiah 8:19–20 KJV)

People always seem to want "quick fixes," especially when it comes to security and prosperity. King Saul was one of those. Even after he had banned seeking after mediums, he sought the advice of the medium of Endor (1 Samuel 28:1–20). Saul recognized the reality of the spirit world, and his efforts to contact a spirit had tragic results for the king.

The Philistines had gathered to war against Israel, and the prophet Samuel was dead. In fear, Saul inquired of the Lord, but there was no answer. Then the king disguised himself and sought counsel from the medium. God stepped in and pronounced judgment against Saul. In the next battle, Saul and his son Jonathan were killed (31:1–6).

Today mediums are called "channelers." They purport to contact the spirits of deceased persons or contact spirits of another realm. The term *famil-*

iar spirit (Isaiah 8:19 KJV, ASV) seems to refer to a family relative or a servant in the household. The medium or channeler supposedly calls up the spirit of the dead. In reality, a knowledgeable demon, who is familiar with the dead person's characteristics and activities, impersonates the dead, deceiving the person desiring to make contact.

When the Israelites were about to invade the Promised Land, God strictly warned them against all occult practices (Deuteronomy 18:9–14). He called them "abominations"; God put them in the same category of "detestable things" (NASB) as infant sacrifice (18:10). All occult practices, such as fortune-telling, magic, and spiritism, are detestable to God. Why should people consult the devil's practitioners rather than the true and living God? The Word of God and counselors who rely on the Bible are sufficient. There is no beginning of light ("no dawn" NASB) in occult counselors (Isaiah 8:20). The Bible consistently condemns such things, and for the sons of Israel severe penalties were prescribed for those guilty of such practices (Leviticus 20:6, 27).

Today, those who have even dabbled in such things need to confess and renounce their sinful inquiries. In Acts 19:18–20, we read that those who practiced magic brought their books and, in the sight of all, burned them. Their price was equivalent to 137 man-year wages, or millions of dollars. This complete break with the occult past needs to be done today.

O true and living God, if I have sought secret information or power such as You have condemned, I repent of all such occasions. I confess this as the sin of rebel-lion, and I stand against it in the name of the Lord Je-sus. Cleanse me of such thinking and keep me from the influence and attacks of the evil one. I submit anew to You, and ask You to guide me away from error and into the paths of righteousness for Your name's sake. I choose not to participate in the works of darkness but rather to expose them. Strengthen me to warn others also. In Jesus' name, amen.

The Devil's Angels

And the King will answer and say . . . to those on His left, "Depart from Me, accursed ones, into the eternal fire which has been prepared for the devil and his angels." (Matthew 25:40–41)

There are some so gullible that they think all angels are good, that they are here to help anyone who calls on them, and that they will guide us unerringly into the path of success, health, and happiness. Thus a California minister has declared that angels can help people work out "unresolved trauma," and a Wisconsin psychiatrist once told a *Newsweek* magazine reporter, "Most people think of angels as being benign, pleasant and helping."

How foolish in the light of God's clear revelation. There are evil angels, masquerading as "angels of light" (2 Corinthians 11:14–15); and many are tricked by this masquerade.

The Lord Jesus recognized the reality of the devil and all his angels. They are active and continually oppose God, His Messiah, and His people. But there will come an end to all that. On that great judgment day, after the defeat of Satan's last attempt to overthrow God and usurp His kingdom, the

Lord Jesus will cast Satan and all his army into the Lake of Fire. What a day of rejoicing that will be! Never again will the devil rear his ugly, evil head to kill and destroy.

During the Great Tribulation period, Michael and his angels will win the battle with the devil and his angels. For a season the evil angels will trouble God's people and the world, but God shall give relief to His afflicted people "when the Lord Jesus shall be revealed from heaven with His mighty angels in flaming fire, dealing out retribution to those who do not know God and to those who do not obey the gospel of our Lord Jesus" (1 Thessalonians 1:8–9). Because the Lord Jesus judged Satan and his angels at the cross, He now limits their evil deeds; and He will remove them finally from the earthly scene. He will cast Satan and all those who followed him, men and angels, into the fire for "eternal punishment" (Matthew 25:46).

Then the Lord Jesus shall reign forever in the new heavens and new earth in which righteousness permanently dwells (2 Peter 3:13; Revelation 21:1–5). Only those who have been cleansed by the blood of the Lamb, the Lord Jesus, shall enjoy the provisions of eternal life. "Outside are the dogs and the sorcerers [magicians] and the immoral persons and the murderers and the idolaters, and everyone who loves and practices lying" (Revelation 22:14–15). What a just and amazing end!

Sovereign Lord Jesus, I am so glad that You have complete control over all, the good and the evil. Nothing escapes Your notice, and nothing can successfully oppose Your plan. You will reign in righteousness, and I

*shall reign eternally with You. I choose to give You com-
plete reign in my life today and forever. Keep me from
the evil one. I praise Your righteousness that judges the
devil and his angels who have brought such evil into the
world. I praise and thank You for Your grace that rescued me and made me a child of Your family and a
member of Your kingdom. Amen.*

Sons of God

> *Now it came about, when men began to multiply
> on the face of the land, and daughters were born to
> them, that the sons of God saw that the daughters of
> men were beautiful; and they took wives for them-
> selves, whomever they chose.* (Genesis 6:1–2)

In chapter 3, page 43, we saw that good angels are
called *sons of God*. There is evidence that evil angels
also bear this name, specifically in the story of the
sons of God who took women as their wives.

The story, found in Genesis 6:1–4, presents a
problem of interpretation. The question is whether
the term *sons of God* refers to humans or to fallen
angels. There is no easy solution. Either position
has some problems, and good men are divided on
the issue.

Those who hold that the sons of God were men
object to the idea that demons can so act in the
human scene to cause women to bear children
without impregnation by a man. Of course, we do
not know all that evil, supernatural beings can do.
They do, however, affect the course of nature. Ob-
jectors also point out that angels are sexless, citing
Jesus' words in Matthew 22:30. The angels indeed
are without gender, but the point the Lord Jesus
was making in this case is that angels do not pro-

create among themselves. Matthew 22:23–33 treats the questions of producing children to retain inheritance rights for the family of a deceased man. It does not say angels cannot play with human procreation. Further, we know that demons can affect the human body. Some suggest that the preceding context of Genesis contrasts the lines of godly Sethites and the ungodly Cainites. But if the Sethites are godly, why would they turn to multiple marriages? And is this cause for God to destroy the whole world through a flood?

It seems preferable to view the *sons of God* as fallen angels. Outside of Genesis 6, the exact term is used only of angels (Job 1:6; 2:1; 38:7; compare Daniel 4:25). Angels have the power to eat, walk, talk, and sit and were mistaken for human men by the homosexuals of Sodom (Genesis 18:1–19:5).

What reason is there for limiting "daughters of men" to ungodly women? Genesis states, "The Nephilim [Hebrew for "fallen ones"] were on the earth in those days," as if this were an unusual visitation. This could be a term to speak of demons. The term *daughters of men,* then, is designed to distinguish human women in general from a class of fallen angels. And why limit just formerly godly men with ungodly women? Couldn't Cainites take wives from Sethite women? And why are the children of this union so unusual? They are "earthborn ones" (Septuagint), a term used of Titans, who were partly gods and partly humans in Greek mythology.

There are other reasons to believe that the phrase *sons of God* is a term for fallen angels. The New Testament seems clearly to refer to the well-known judgment of these fallen angels in 2 Peter 2:4–5 and Jude 6–7. The reference to the gross immorality of Sodom and Gomorrah and the connection to the flood requires a clear scriptural record of judgment upon these angels who did not remain in their own estate but went after alien flesh. All these angels were bound without release until final judgment. This, then, cannot be the original fall of angels with Satan; otherwise, how would Satan and his angels be active on earth today, as is the picture in the New Testament? This must have been a wretched and race-damaging sin that was partly the cause for the worldwide flood.

The actions of such diabolical angels would explain Moses' words about the Flood being a universal judgment upon the wickedness of men and evil angels: "The Lord saw that the wickedness of man was great on the earth, and that every intent of the thoughts of his heart was only evil continually" (Genesis 6:5). Humans had continued in their self-centered way of life, and they allowed demons to cohabit with womenkind. I believe these demons attempted to pollute the race and to prevent the Lord Jesus from becoming truly human to be our Kinsman Redeemer. God had to intervene; judgment was needed.

The whole series of events may seem foreboding, but the apostle Peter encourages us with these thoughts: If God spared not these angels, not the ancient world, nor the cities of Sodom and Gomorrah, and if He rescued Lot, then "the Lord knows how to rescue the godly from temptation, and to keep the unrighteous under punishment for the day of judgment" (2 Peter 2:9).

Holy Father, I thank You that You are the judge of all—humans and angels. You can handle even gross attempts of our foes to pollute the human race and to interfere with Your plan of redemption. When I consider the evil schemes of the devil, I am confident that You can keep me through the strong grace of the Lord Jesus. I commit myself to You afresh. In Jesus' name, amen.

Spirits in Prison

For Christ also died for sins once for all, the just for the unjust, so that He might bring us to God, having been put to death in the flesh, but made alive in the spirit; in which also He went and made proclamation to the spirits now in prison, who once were disobedient, when the patience of God kept waiting in the days of Noah. . . . (1 Peter 3:18–20a)

Like Genesis 6:1–6 and its discussion of the sons of God, a passage in 1 Peter has evoked controversy over the meaning of a phrase. Who are the *spirits now in prison* of 1 Peter 3:19? Did Christ preach the gospel to the lost men of all ages when He descended into hades to give them a second chance to be saved? Or did Christ, through the Holy Spirit in Noah, preach to men of Noah's day?

The Bible holds out no hope for those who have died never having trusted God who saves lost humans through Jesus Christ. Jesus Himself said, "unless you believe that I am He, you shall die in your sins" (John 8:24). He also said, "He who believes in the Son has eternal life; but he who does not obey the Son shall not see life, but the wrath of God abides on him" (John 3:36). Hebrews 9:27 reads, "It is appointed for men to die once and after this comes judgment." There is not a shred of evidence for a "second chance." These scriptural statements, along with its teaching of resurrection of the human body, also rule out any thought of reincarnation. It is in this life that we must choose to trust Christ or face the eternal judgment of God.

The context of 1 Peter 3 indicates that this preaching by Christ was done, not in Noah's era, but in the interval between Christ's death and resurrection. The sequence of events is that Christ was "put to death," "made alive in spirit," "went," "made proclamation," and then rose and ascended, as indicated by "having gone into heaven." If this proclaiming was done by Christ between His death and resurrection, what was it all about?

It seems best to understand that the Lord Jesus, after He died, went in His spirit to make a victory announcement to those fallen angels who had sinned in Noah's day. These spirits are also called "sons of God" who caused unusual progeny through impregnating "the daughters of men" (Genesis 6:1–4). In effect He seems to have said, "You sought to interfere with My Kinsman-Redeemer role when you tried to pollute the race, making it less than completely human. But now I have completed God's purpose, I have shed my blood, I have died as the God-man for the race of sinners. And in the process, I have condemned and judged you and all of Satan's angels." What a proclamation!

To support this, we note that the word *spirits*, when used in the New Testament without further description, always refers to angels or demons. Peter would know that there were angelic *spirits in prison*, as shown in 2 Peter 2:4 when he says about sinning angels that God "cast them into hell (tartarus) and committed them to pits of darkness, reserved for judgment." In 1 Peter 3, the apostle uses the term "herald" or "proclaim," not "to preach the gospel." This is a victory pronouncement. Christ has conquered the hosts of evil! Angels have been in view in the whole context, it seems clear, from the reference in verse 22: "who is at the right hand of God, having gone into heaven, after angels and authorities and powers had been subjected to Him."

The theme of 1 Peter is "the sufferings . . . and the glories to follow" (1:11). If we follow Christ's example and encounter sufferings—as He, the righteous one, died to pay the penalty for our sins—we also have glory waiting for us. In the meantime, Christ is sovereignly controlling all events, human and angelic; for God subjected all the universe to the God-man, our Redeemer. We can trust Him to see us through whatever befalls us in the course of our lives. How good it is to know that one day Christ will rescue us from the very presence of evil and will deliver us safely into His kingdom. To die in this day, to be absent from our bodies, is to be at home with the Lord (2 Corinthians 5:8). It is also good to know that in a future day, Christ will raise us in glorified bodies (1 Corinthians 15:20–23) and will send Satan and his armies to the Lake of Fire (Matthew 25:41).

Dear Savior, I thank You for suffering the penalty due mankind and due me. I trust You and You alone for forgiveness of my sins. I'm so glad that You have by Your death and resurrection conquered all the hosts of Satan and that they will be finally removed from the earthly scene. You allowed him to bruise Your heel, but You certainly crushed his head! Please crush Satan under our heels soon. Keep me true and faithful, depending on You and Your Spirit to enable me in every good motive and effort until I see You face-to-face. Help me also to share the good news of Your salvation with many. I praise You for Your grace and power. Amen.

Chapter 10

ANGELS IN THE BOOK OF REVELATION

The book of Revelation came from the risen Lord Jesus Christ, "and He sent and communicated it by His angel to His bond-servant John" (1:1). The apostle John was exiled to the island of Patmos because of His fearless witness to the Lord Jesus (1:9). While there, he received the Lord's orders to write a summary of his visions from Christ.

The revelation to John of future things in this final book of the Bible included both messages to the early church and the church at the end of the age (Revelation 1:19). Angels announced and depicted events present and future.

An interpreting angel helped the apostle understand the vision. Other angels appear in Revelation as individuals or groups. We have already considered (in chapter 4) the Living Creatures of Revelation, who worship and praise God and are active in directing His judgments during the Great Tribulation. Five other groups are involved in events described in the Revelation of John:

- Messengers of the Seven Churches
- Four Angels of the Four Winds
- Seven Angels of the Seven Trumpets
- Seven Angels of Seven Plagues
- Twenty-Four Elders in Heaven

Messengers of the Seven Churches

Write in a book what you see, and send it to the seven churches. . . . As for the mystery of the seven stars which you saw in My right hand, and the seven golden lampstands: the seven stars are the angels of the seven churches, and the seven lampstands are the seven churches. (Revelation 1:11, 20)

Seven churches in Asia Minor were undergoing temptations and persecution. The seven churches were located in Ephesus, Smyrna, Pergamum, Thyatira, Sardis, Philadelphia, and Laodicea; and part of the apostle John's visions involved the things pertaining to the life and witness of these seven churches (Revelation 1:11; 2, 3). John was to write letters to these churches by writing to the angel (messenger) of each church.

In John's vision of Revelation 1, which was addressed to these seven churches, he saw the Lord Jesus in an unusual human form (1:13–14). This awesome person was clothed as a priest "and in His right hand He held seven stars" (1:16). The sight of his glorious Lord caused him to fall "at His feet as a dead man" (1:17).

What or who were these seven stars? The Lord Jesus clarified this to John and to us in Revelation 1:20: "As for the mystery of the seven stars which you saw in My right hand, and the seven golden lampstands; the seven stars are *the angels of the seven churches*, and the seven lampstands are the seven churches" (italics added).

Still the question remains: Are these spirit beings assigned to the churches or are they human messengers involved in the life of each church? Remember, the word *angelos* means messenger. It is clearly used of both spirit beings and humans. It was used of John the Baptist (Mark 1:2), John's messengers (Luke 7:24), Jesus' messengers (Luke 9:52), and of the spies who hid in Rahab's house (James 2:25). However, the word is used mostly of spirit beings; and except for Revelation 2 and 3, there is little question as to what sort of beings are meant.

The evidence is not sufficient to come to a definite conclusion. In favor of the angel view, we note the preponderance of the use of *angelos* is of spirit beings, particularly in the context of the book of Revelation. Further, "stars" have been a symbolic representation for angels several places in Scripture. (See page 47 for the use of "stars" as angels.) Some think the responsibilities are too great for a man and leadership had not sufficiently advanced to the point where one man could be considered the leader for each church at the time of writing. However, there were capable leaders of the churches by the time of the Lord's half brother James in Jerusalem (Acts 15:12–21) and by the time of Paul (Acts 14:19–23).

In favor of the view that these "angels" were human messengers, we could understand that John was to write to specific messengers involved in the life of each church to deal with concrete problems they were facing. Writing to a spirit being does not seem to be a direct way of handling these matters, and there is a problem having an angelic postal delivery service. There were humans who kept contact with John on Patmos.

Lord Jesus, head of the church and Lord of the churches, I recognize You as the Lord of my life. Incline my heart to listen to Your words of correction and encouragement that I might obey You and honor You in all circumstances of my life. Amen.

Four Angels of the Four Winds

After this I saw four angels standing at the four corners of the earth, holding back the four winds of the earth, so that no wind would blow on the earth or on the sea or on any tree. (Revelation 7:1)

We continue with the visions of John regarding future things in the Great Tribulation, "for the great day of their wrath [God's and the Lamb's] has come; and who is able to stand?" (6:17). In Revelation 7:1, John "saw *four angels* standing at the four corners of the earth, *holding back the four winds of the earth* so that no wind should blow on the earth or on the sea or on any tree" (italics added). This was ordered so as to not to "harm the earth or the sea or the trees until we have sealed the bond-servants of our God on their foreheads" (7:3).

God is concerned for the physical protection of His witnesses during the Great Tribulation. These witnesses from the twelve tribes of Israel have a special task to witness for the Lord Jesus during this period of God's great judgment. They must not be hurt so that they may complete their assignment. Evidently they will be protected, for the following scene pictures an innumerable multitude from every nation coming to wash their robes white in the blood of the Lamb (Revelation 7:9–17).

So these four angels hold back God's judgment, symbolized by the four winds from the four corners of the earth. We should not suppose that the Bible presents a flat earth with four corners. Today we also speak figuratively of the four compass points of the earth. The idea is that angelic control, used but not needed by God, is sufficient and extends to controlling the elements in this case.

Earlier Scriptures have shown that God allows angels sometimes to control nature. In the book of Job, we read that Satan caused a great wind to destroy the house of Job's children (Job 1:12, 18–19). Previously a fire fell from heaven and burned up Job's flocks and the shepherds (1:16). In Revelation 16:8, we read of one angel who will cause an increase in the heat of the sun, 93 million miles from the earth, so that humans are scorched with its fire.

Angels have great power in this world. But we do not need to fear God's holy angels, for their power is granted by God and governed by God. Neither would they want to harm God's loved ones. We can rest in God's sovereign care. We can also thank Him for the role that angels play in our protection and provision. How good to have powerful angels operating behind the scenes on our behalf. Have you ever thanked the Lord for them? Have you ever asked Him for angelic protection? Such angelic help would not be out of keeping with His revelation or His way of governing.

Lord God, I thank You that through faith in the Lord Jesus I am Your child. I thank You also for the protection and provision You give to Your children. If it were not for You, I would have perished long ago in the events of nature and by the attacks of the supernatural. Through Your angels continue to protect me. I trust You for the direction of my life and service to You, and I will serve You completely. Amen.

Seven Angels of the Seven Trumpets

And when He broke the seventh seal, there was silence in heaven for about half an hour. And I saw the seven angels who stand before God; and seven trumpets were given to them. (Revelation 8:1–2)

The seven angels described in Revelation 8 do not have specific names, but they obviously hold great position and authority in God's scheme of things. "To them were given seven trumpets to call for judgment on the earth" (Revelation 8:2). These messengers have control over the earth during the Great Tribulation to bring the wrath of God to bear upon those "earth-dwellers" opposed to God and to His Messiah (3:10).

In Revelation 8:6–12, we see a sequence of severe judgments. When the first angel sounded his trumpet, hail and fire, mixed with blood, was thrown upon the earth; and one-third of all vegetation was destroyed. The second angel sounded his trumpet and caused one-third of the seas to become blood. As a result, one-third of the sea creatures were destroyed along with one-third of the ships. The third angel caused a burning star to fall upon the earth (meteor?) to make one-third of the fresh waters bitter, so that many humans died. The fourth angel sounded a trumpet, and one-third of the sun, moon, and stars were darkened, shortening the lighted part of the day and night.

The next three judgments caused by the angels are called "woes," because these judgments will be even harsher in their severity than the first four

(8:13). The fifth angel loosed what seems to be a horde of demons who were limited to tormenting humans who did not have God's seal of protection (9:1–11). The sixth angel sounded a trumpet, and a voice from before God said, "Release the four angels who are bound at the great river Euphrates" (9:14). When those demonic spirits were released, they destroyed with fire and smoke and brimstone one-third of mankind. Still those who were not killed did not repent of their worship of idols and demons nor of their magic or immorality (8:17–21).

The seventh angel completed the trumpet judgments and introduced the judgments of the seven bowls. God's judgments keep on intensifying, preparing the way for the return of the Lord Jesus in glory to reign on earth (10:7). When the seventh angel sounded his trumpet, "there were loud voices in heaven, saying, 'The kingdom of the world has become the kingdom of our Lord, and of His Christ [Messiah] and He will reign forever and ever'" (11:15). Heaven's response is thanks to the Almighty, the eternal God, "because Thou hast taken Thy great power and hast begun to reign" (11:17). The nations were enraged, but God's wrath will destroy those who destroy His earth (11:18).

How terrifying the spectacle! When God moves his holy angels to judge the earth, there will be no place to hide. Yet millions still will not repent. Many are saved during the Great Tribulation (Revelation 7:9–17), yet the majority of mankind, the earth-dwellers who have followed the Antichrist and Satan, will perish during the Tribulation and at the Lord's return to earth to judge and to rule (19:11–21).

How good to have the promise that those who belong to His genuine body of believers, the church, will not even be present during this great time of God's wrath. This wrath is designed to come upon "those who dwell on the earth," or earth-dwellers, a term used six times in Revelation to describe the followers of the Antichrist and Satan (3:10). We who now believe in the Lord Jesus will be kept from that very time, not just hidden from the wrath around us. Such is the force of Jesus' promise in Revelation 3:10: "I also will keep you from [Greek, *tereso ek*, to guard from] the hour of testing, that hour which is about to . . . test those who dwell upon the earth [earth-dwellers]." Those who truly trust in Jesus shall never experience those ferocious judgments leveled by the seven angels of the seven trumpets.

In 1974, our family visited the World's Fair in Spokane, Washington. The theme of the U.S. pavilion was "The Earth Does Not Belong to Man. Man Belongs to the Earth." Nothing could be farther from the truth. While man was given the responsibility to care for the earth, it belongs to God. Man belongs to God, and the earth belongs to God. He has a right to judge all who do not properly submit to Him and His righteous rule. So God will destroy much of the earth and of mankind because of sin and rebellion. God does not worship ecology, and neither should we. The religious teaching that says we originated from the earth, either by natural evolution or by spirit involvement, is contrary to the revealed Word of our Creator God.

We belong to the true and living God, maker of heaven and earth. We are to care for the earth and for mankind as stewards of God's rule and grace. But we are never to substitute "mother earth" for our Father God.

During these seven judgments that assail the earth, God will be in control. In His wisdom, He will do what is right and just, and these seven angels will be part of that wise judgment.

Thank You, righteous and sovereign Father God, that you do all things well. You are gracious and good; yet You must judge evil to be true to yourself and your role as ruler of the universe. Thank You for sending your Son to take my judgment that I should never have to face your judgment. Help me to trust you with my life and welfare and to fulfill the responsibilities you have assigned me in the church and in the world. Amen.

Seven Angels of the Seven Plagues

Then I saw another sign in heaven, great and marvelous, seven angels who had seven plagues, which are the last, because in them the wrath of God is finished. (Revelation 15:1)

Revelation 15 pictures "seven angels who had seven plagues." These are the last plagues of the Great Tribulation, "because in them the wrath of God is finished" (15:1). After the redeemed of the Tribulation sing the song of Moses and the song of the Lamb praising God's righteous judgments, "one of the four living creatures gave to the seven angels seven golden bowls full of the wrath of God, who lives forever and ever" (15:7). A voice from the temple of God commands them to pour out their wrath on the earth.

The first angel poured out his bowl and caused malignant sores upon all the earth-dwellers "who had the mark of the beast and who worshiped his image" (Revelation 16:2). The second angel poured out his bowl into the sea and it became like blood so that all life in the sea perished (16:3). The third poured out his bowl into the fresh waters, and they became as blood. This angel praised God for His righteous judgment, because men deserved it (16:4–6). The fourth angel caused the sun to scorch men with fire. They blasphemed God and did not repent; such is the hardness of the sinners' hearts (16:8–9)! The fifth angel attacked the throne of the Antichrist, "and his kingdom became darkened; and they gnawed their tongues because of pain." Yet they blasphemed God and did not repent (16:10–11).

The sixth angel poured out his bowl on the river Euphrates, drying it up so that the kings of the east could come against Israel. All the kings of the earth were empowered by demons to enter the battle of Har-Magedon [Armageddon] where God shall bring them utter and final defeat (16:12–16).

Finally, the seventh angel poured his bowl into the air. A voice from the throne said, "It is done." Then lightning, thunder, and the greatest of all earthquakes hit the earth. Babylon, representing the center of politico-religious rebellion against God, fell under the great wrath of God. The leading demonically controlled world system now receives her just punishment. Huge one-hundred-pound hailstones pummel the earth, the topography drastically changes, and still men blaspheme God and do not repent (16:17–21).

How horrible the waste and carnage! How thorough God's righteous judgments! Yet how adamant, how fiercely defiant, how senseless is man's continued rebellion against God! It cannot be explained only by mankind's depravity. It is driven by demons who dominate those who worship false gods and Satan. Our humanistic, materialistic, and rationalistic worldview must be discarded for the biblical worldview that recognizes the reality of God and the spirit world. It is time for us to repent of our unspiritual concepts and turn to the true and living God for His perspective and insight.

Thank You, holy Father, that You cannot allow sin and wickedness to continue forever. Thank You that in the proper time You will end all unrighteousness on the earth. If I have seriously questioned Your ways, forgive me. I repent of my limited view of truth, my fear, and my stubbornness that keeps me from the best You have for me. Give me perspective and insight that will guide me to honor You and serve others. In Jesus' name, amen.

Twenty-Four Elders in Heaven

Immediately I was in the Spirit; and behold, a throne was standing in heaven, and One sitting on the throne. . . . and upon the thrones I saw twenty-four elders sitting clothed in white garments, and golden crowns on their heads. (Revelation 4:2, 4)

How can twenty-four elders be listed as angels? you may wonder. The elders are described in Revelation 4 and 5, and commentators divide on who these twenty-four elders are. Some say that the elders represent the true church of Christ as it appears in heaven, but a case can be made that they are angels.

Let's first consider the view that the "twenty-four elders" represent Christ's church as it appears in heaven, having been delivered from the Great Tribulation occurring on earth. As the word "elders" in the New Testament refers to officers and representatives in the local church, these commentators believe that must be their identity. In addition, they believe the mention of crowns and of ruling on thrones refers to believers' rewards and privileges.

Other Bible commentators, however, hold that the twenty-four elders are actually angels. These angels attend God in priestly fashion at His throne along with the "four living creatures," whom we have identified as spirit beings.

To support this view, we see the elders joining the four living beings to praise God for the redemption of mankind in an expression that seems to exclude themselves. Significant biblical manuscripts omit "us" in Revelation 5:9 and read "them" and "they" instead of "us and we" in 5:10. (This is the reading in the *New International Version,* for example.) If the pronouns are third person *they* and *them,* then those twenty-four elders are describing believers in God's kingdom; and the "elders" are angels. At times, angels have appeared in white robes and they may act as God's appointed representatives for His redeemed people on earth. (For examples, see Daniel 12:1; Matthew 18:10; Luke 1:19; Revelation 8:3.) As representatives of God's people, these angels may number twenty-four, some believe, to correspond to the twenty-four courses of priests set by King David (1 Chronicles 24) and to the sum of the twelve tribes and the twelve apostles.

Though there is not sufficient evidence to come to a definite conclusion as to whether these are redeemed humans or angels, we can see the devotion of these twenty-four to the praise and adoration of God as Creator (Revelation 4:11) and Christ as Redeemer (5:8–12). However, it seems most likely that the twenty-four elders are angels who join with the four living beings to say, "To Him who sits on the throne, and to the Lamb, be blessing and honor and glory and dominion forever and ever" (5:13).

What privilege is ours to know the truth of God's Word and to see that His truth is centered in the Lord Jesus Christ! We too should worship the true and living God as the Creator of all and the Lamb of God as the Redeemer of all who trust in Him. And like every created thing in heaven and earth and under the earth and on the sea that responded to the worship of the living beings and the twenty-four elders, we too can say, "Amen!"

For the privilege that I, along with fellow believers, have to know the truth and to be eternally related to the Son of God, I thank You and worship You. You are the sovereign Creator and Redeemer. Blessing, honor, glory, and power belong to You now in my life and forever. Amen.

Epilogue
NAME ABOVE ALL NAMES

And He is the radiance of His glory and the exact representation of His nature, and upholds all things by the word of His power. When He had made purification of sins, He sat down at the right hand of the Majesty on high, having become as much better than the angels, as He has inherited a more excellent name than they. For to which of the angels did He ever say, "You are My Son, today I have begotten You?" And again, "I will be a Father to Him, and He shall be a Son to Me?" (Hebrews 1:3–5)

Many names may be applied to angels. Some of the names they wear are great and awe-inspiring. They are magnificent beings, created directly by the hand of God. We can respect and appreciate them and their ministries. However, none of them can ever be called *Son of God*. The Lord Jesus, the Messiah, is the one and only Son of God. His is the name above every other (Philippians 2:9).

The apostle John calls Him "only begotten." The Greek word used means "one and only," "one of a kind," "unique." The Son is genuine God, the fullness of deity in human, bodily form (Colossians 2:9). He is eternal with the Father and was sent to become genuinely human as well (John 1:1–2, 14). Jesus Himself said, "He who has seen me has seen the Father. . . . Do you not believe that I am in the

Father, and the Father is in Me?" (John 14:9b–10a).

The writer of Hebrews explains that no angel was ever or will ever be called "Son." All angels are created beings. Even though they never die, they are not eternal. Instead, God commands, "Let all the angels of God worship Him" (Hebrews 1:6). Not even Michael, the only one named "archangel," is exempt. He, too, despite some cultic notions, must worship another called "Son."

We have seen that angels are called "sons of God," as belonging to a class of strong ones that never die. But Jesus is called Jehovah God. The apostle Paul asserts this by quoting Isaiah 45:22–24. In Philippians 2:5–11, he writes that God, who sent His Son to take on human form to die for us, has now "highly exalted Him, and has bestowed on Him the name which is above every name, that at the name of Jesus every knee should bow, of those who are in heaven, and on earth, and under the earth, and that every tongue should confess that Jesus Christ is Lord [the equivalent of Jehovah, or *Yaweh*], to the glory of God the Father" (2:9–11). This includes all angels and all humans.

No angel has the right to be worshiped (Exodus 20:1–6). In fact, angels strongly forbid such action themselves (Revelation 19:10; 22:9). The Bible warns against any worshiping of angels whatever (Colossians 2:18). We, along with the holy angels, have the privilege and responsibility to worship the one true Son. We are to honor Him just as we honor the Father. To do less is to dishonor both God and Christ (John 5:22–23). He is not only the Son of God, but He is the only mediator between God and all men (1 Timothy 2:5). He is the only Savior.

Have you made Jesus the Lord your Savior and Lord? If you are uncertain, why not receive Him right now? Simply believe He is God's perfect Son and your Savior from sin; and ask Him to enter your life (John 1:12; Romans 10:9–10). If you trust Him, He will forgive your sins and rightly relate you to God for time and eternity. That's why the Son became man. He loves us and gave himself for us. Receiving Him, you will pass from death to life and from darkness to light (John 5:24). You will spend your life here and your life in eternity with God's one and only Son, who is so much greater than any angel.

Dear Father, I do trust You for Your forgiveness and I look forward to spending all my days with You. Thank You, dear Son of God, for Your sacrifice as God-man in my place. Thank You, Father, for making me a son (or a daughter) of Yours, perfectly accepted in Your special Son. Thank you, Holy Spirit, for making the truth about the Son real to me. Along with all the holy angels, I worship the Triune God, and You alone. Keep me from deception and lead me in the truth of Your Word. You are my Creator, Redeemer, and friend; and I rejoice to be Your child forever. Magnify Your grace in me. In Jesus' magnificent, saving name I pray. Amen.

SUBJECT
INDEX

SCRIPTURE INDEX

Moody Press, a ministry of Moody Bible Institute,
is designed for education, evangelization, and edification.
If we may assist you in knowing more about Christ
and the Christian life, please write us without obligation:
Moody Press, c/o MLM, Chicago, Illinois 60610.